W9-DER-531

Interstate Cooperation

Interstate Cooperation

A STUDY OF THE INTERSTATE COMPACT

By Vincent V. Thursby

Associate Professor of Political Science,
Florida State University

Introduction by Carl B. Swisher

Public Affairs Press, Washington, D. C.

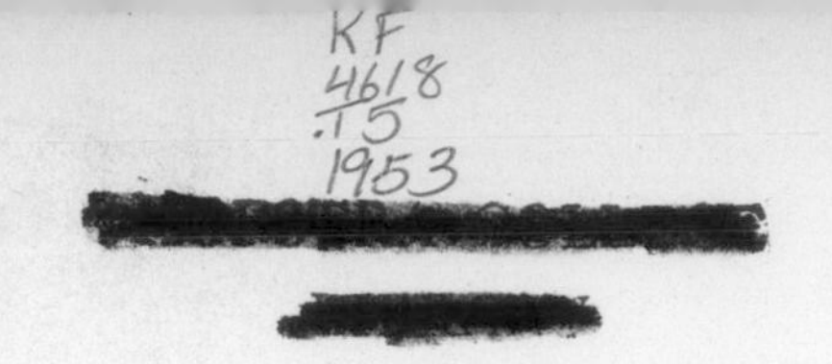

PREFACE

"No State shall, without the consent of Congress, . . . enter into any agreement or compact with another State or with a foreign power. . . ." This, the Compact Clause of the Constitution of the United States, is the subject of this study. It is primarily a study in public law.

The interstate compact affords one means of rendering area coincident with function. It may be the only means on many matters whereby effective cooperative action between or among the States can be achieved which will at the same time preserve the vitality and potency of the States and avoid the imposition of an excessive burden upon the general government. The compact device merits consideration with an eye cocked to determination of its possible role in the federal system.

To Professors James Hart and George W. Spicer of the University of Virginia the author owes a real debt of gratitude. Their counsel and suggestions were most encouraging. For sins of omission or commission, of course, the author must accept full responsibility.

Quotations appearing in this book are reprinted by permission of James H. Allen, Edward S. Corwin, Edwin R. Cotton, Wayne D. Heydecker, J. G. Randall, Appleton-Century-Crofts, Alfred A. Knopf, American Society for Public Administration, American Political Science Association, American Academy of Political and Social Science, Baker, Voorhis & Co., Columbia University Press, *Cornell Law Quarterly*, Council of State Governments, Foundation Press, *Fortune*, G. P. Putnam's Sons, Harcourt Brace and Co., *Harper's Magazine*, Henry Holt and Co., *Iowa Law Review*, Little, Brown and Co., Macmillan Co., McGraw-Hill, *Marquette Law Review*, D. C. Heath and Co., Oxford University Press, *Political Science Quarterly*, Princeton University Press, Office of Education, Federal Security Agency, *University of Chicago Law Review*, University of Chicago Press, University of North Carolina Press, *Vanderbilt Law Review*, Viking Press, *Virginia Law Review*, and the *Yale Law Review*. Their kindness is appreciated.

VINCENT V. THURSBY

2153 Florida Avenue, Washington 8, D. C.

Printed in the United States of America
Library of Congress Card No. 53-5792

INTRODUCTION

The expanding responsibilities of government in the United States require perennial search for new working devices and for new ways of using old ones. Although government at local levels is doing a far greater total of work than ever before, the tendency toward centralization of power and responsibility in the federal government reflects a decline in our relative ability to cope with problems at local levels. Yet drastic centralization has evils and defects all its own. It removes financial and political responsibility for good government from the people most directly affected and lodges it in a distant bureaucracy. It makes representative democracy at once less democratic and less representative. It oftentimes saddles the federal government with responsibilities which, although extending beyond the lines of an individual state, are yet so peculiarly local that administration from Washington violates the canons of federalism. At most, the problems involved may be regional rather than national. Although the federal government has done much and will do still more to adjust national administration to regional differences, no central government can avoid some loss of the "common touch" in managing for them the infinitely diverse problems of multiple localities. In the light of this fact we seek devices for keeping government local without limiting it to individual states when the problems involved cut across state lines and so defy individual state solutions.

In this volume Dr. Thursby has made a thorough and illuminating study and appraisal of the interstate compact, one of the devices by which we resist the extremes of centralization while providing for the over-all coping with local problems cutting across the boundaries of two or more states. The device as conceived by the framers of the Constitution had admitted dangers, in that, unless properly restrained, it might enable particular groups of states to combine to the injury of other states. The framers solved this problem by forbidding the making of interstate compacts without the consent of Congress. Congress, in other words, must sit in judgment on any compact that two or more states may propose. The device has limitations, particularly in that, while it may be effective for settling disputed state boundaries or setting up machinery for performing a great variety of clearly prescribed functions, a mere compact between or among sovereign states is not a good base for an organization which must make policy and evolve program as it goes along. But within the limits of its possibilities the interstate compact is performing an increasingly important function in the handling of problems which without its use would go partly unsolved or be transferred to the jurisdiction of the federal government. The importance of the device punctuates the value of the comprehensive study which Dr. Thursby has made of the law, the facts, and the literature dealing with its use. The study will have a high rating among monographs dealing with the techniques of adapting governmental machinery to the pressures of modern needs.

CARL BRENT SWISHER

CONTENTS

CHAPTER I

THE SETTING

The primary concern of this study is the Compact Clause of the Constitution in public law. Preliminary to launching into an investigation of this field, however, it is necessary to attempt some exposition of the more general considerations which appertain to the Compact Clause. Understanding of the potentialities of the Compact Clause will embrace the knowledge that it is one means of resolving interstate conflicts and one means of tackling supra-state, sub-national problems. There are others essential to the context within which the compact device must be conceived.

Interstate Conflicts and the Compact Device. The Constitution makes provisions for two methods of adjustment or settlement of problems transcending state lines. One is the grant to the Supreme Court of jurisdiction over controversies between two or more States, and the other is the authorization for interstate compacts with the consent of Congress.[1]

American experience prior to the Declaration of Independence in 1776 and under the Articles of Confederation pointed to the need for some provision in the Constitution as to final settlement of interstate disputes over jurisdiction, boundaries, waters, and comparable matters. Before severance of the American colonies from England, power was lodged in the King's Privy Council to determine any questions arising under Royal charters as to boundaries. Each of the Colonies was related directly to the Crown, and inter-colonial disputes were submitted for resolution to the common superior, the King in Council.[2] Thus, in 1727, the Privy Council decided a boundary case instituted by Rhode Island against Connecticut, in 1740, one instituted by New Hampshire against Massachusetts, and, in 1746, one instituted by Rhode Island against Massachusetts.[3] The Colonists were cognizant of these cases and of the need for a court of "last resort" to settle any similar ones which might arise. Hence, it was provided in the Articles of Confederation that "The united states in congress assembled shall . . . be the last resort on appeal in all disputes and differences now subsisting or that hereafter may arise between two or more states concerning boundary, jurisdiction or any other cause whatever. . . ."[4] This power was to be exercised by a court, the members of which were to be chosen by the interested States, or, in the event of their disagreement, from a panel selected by Congress. ". . . the judgment and sentence of the court to be appointed . . . shall be final and conclusive; and if any of the parties shall refuse to submit to the authority of such court, or to appear or defend their claim or cause, the court shall nevertheless proceed to pronounce sentence, or judgment, which shall in like manner be final and decisive, the judgment or sentence and other proceedings being in either case transmitted to congress, and lodged among the acts of congress for the security of the parties concerned. . . ."[5] Three such courts were appointed under the Articles of Confederation in connection with disputes arising between Massachusetts and New York, South Carolina and Georgia, and Connecticut and Pennsylvania. The first two of these were resolved by compacts.[6]

Provisions as to state agreements with foreign powers and as to interstate agreements were incorporated in the Articles of Confederation as follows: "No state without the Consent of the united states in congress assembled, shall . . . enter into any conference, agreement, or alliance or treaty with any King, prince or state. . . . No two or more states shall enter into any treaty, confederation or alliance whatever between them, without the consent of the united states in congress assembled, specifying accurately the purposes for which the same is to be entered into, and how long it shall continue."[7] Story points out with respect to these that manifestly the former clause relates exclusively to foreign states or nations, while the latter relates to the States of the Union.[8] The lack of power in the courts appointed or in Congress to enforce the decrees of the courts became apparent in connection with the judicial settlement of the third boundary dispute — that between Connecticut and Pennsylvania. Madison stated relative thereto in the Federal Constitutional Convention: "Have we not seen the public land dealt out to Cont. to bribe her acquiescence in the decree constitutionally awarded agst. her claim on the territory of Pena.—? for no other possible motive can account for the policy of Congs. in that measure? — if we recur to the examples of other confederacies, we shall find in all of them the same tendency of the parts to encroach on the authority of the whole."[9] Thus, Madison was critical of the Patterson Plan for the new Constitution not only because it omitted "a controul over the States as a general defence of the federal prerogatives," but also because it gave to the federal tribunal "an appellate jurisdiction only."[10] "The plan of Mr. Patterson, not giving even a negative on the Acts of the States, left them as much at liberty as ever to execute their unrighteous projects agst. each other," he said.[11] For a period in the Convention, however, the arrangement prevailed whereby controversies between States with regard to "Jurisdn or Territory" were to be settled by special courts to be selected by Congress by a procedure similar to that under the Articles of Confederation.[12] But this provision was dropped after debate and vote.[13] Rutledge pointed out that, although "this provision was necessary under the Confederation," it "will be rendered unnecessary by the National Judiciary now to be established. . . ."[14] The Framers were aware that a permanent court and power to enforce its decrees were necessary for the settlement of interstate disputes.[15] Hence it was ultimately decided that the Supreme Court should be given, and it was given, jurisdiction "in controversies between two or more states."[16]

In the Federal Convention of 1787, the States created a common superior for certain purposes in the form of a central government. One of the organs of that government, the Supreme Court, was given jurisdiction over appeals from the courts of the States in cases involving federal matters and original jurisdiction over controversies between the States. Moreover, the Court was given jurisdiction over controversies to which the United States was a party. As James Brown Scott notes, the superior was not found already in existence, but was created by "voluntary contract" of the States.[17] The existence of the Court has been significant in the matter of prompting States to resort to the compact device. A noted student of the Supreme Court has stated: "The mere fact of the existence of the Court, with its mighty jurisdiction, has not only encouraged a habit on the part of the States of resorting to it for a decision of their controversies, but it has also encouraged an equally important habit of settling such controversies out of Court, by means of compacts entered into between States."[18] Moreover, the Court, on occasion, has urged litigant States to resort to compacts rather than suits to resolve their disagreements.[19]

Constitutional Basis for Compacts. Writing of the evidences of the "distracted and disheartening condition of the Union," which had deprived it of respect and confidence at home and abroad, Madison stated:

"In certain cases the authy. of the confederacy was disregarded, as in violations not only of the Treaty of peace; but of Treaties with France & Holland, which were complained of to Congs.

"In other cases the Fedl authy was violated by Treaties & wars with Indians, as by Geo: by troops, raised & kept up. witht. the consent of Congs. as by Massts by compacts witht. the consent of Congs. as between Pena. and N. Jersey. and between Virga. & Maryd. From the Legisl: Journals of Virga. it appears, that a vote to apply for a sanction of Congs. was followed by a vote agst. a communication of the Compact to Congs."[20]

Madison then observed that "there had always been some not unfavorable to a partition of the Union into several Confederacies (Marshall's life); either from a better chanc of figuring on a Sectional Theatre, or that the Sections would require stronger Govts. or by their hostile conflicts lead to a monarchical consolidation. The idea of a dismemberment had recently made its appearance in the Newspapers."[21] It was to correct these "defects" and "ominous prospects," Madison said, that the Convention was called. His comments point to the political considerations which account for the inclusion of the Compact Clause. Without it the Federal Government might well have been endangered through political combinations of the States. Certainly, that Government would be interested, too, in a boundary change which would greatly enhance the political power of any one of the States, even though that change might have been effected by interstate agreement. And indeed the general government might be wary of agreements between its individual member-States and foreign powers, which might tend to wean those States from the Union. Yet, the Framers were exceedingly reticent about avowing these considerations.[22] Although the provision was before the Convention several times, it was never debated. There was some discussion as to the propriety of prohibiting the States' levy of tonnage duties (a prohibition included in the same subsection) but none as to that of the Compact Clause.[23] Finally, the restrictions imposed on the States by the Articles as to entering into "any conference, agreement, alliance, or treaty with any foreign power" or into "any treaty, confederation, or alliance whatever between them" without the consent of Congress were adopted in the Constitution in what Charles Warren has chosen to term "a broader form."[24] Subsection 3 of Section 10 of Article I of the Constitution provides: "No State shall, without the consent of Congress, . . . enter into any agreement or compact with another State, or with a foreign power. . . ."[25] The provision apparently was deemed not particularly controversial by the writers of the *Federalist*, who dismissed it with mere restatement of the subsection. This was one of the "particulars of this clause" which "fall within reasonings which are . . . so obvious . . . that they may be passed over without remark."[26] Apparently, too, there was no discussion of "agreements" or "compacts" in any of the state conventions ratifying the Constitution.[27]

The Compact Clause was taken over essentially from that in the Articles of Confederation. And, as has been indicated, the one in the Articles was the outgrowth of the Colonial practice of resolving boundary disputes by means of joint commissions whose decisions were subject to approval by the Crown. It has been stated that the element of congressional consent for compacts between States represents the "republican transformation of the needed approval by the Crown." [28]

Supra-State, Sub-National Considerations and the Element of Congressional Consent. The compact devices have been described as "short circuits" in the nation's federal pattern. As such they are violative of the "'pure' theory of federalism" in that they bring into contact governmental units supposedly "theoretically insulated" from one another. "The Constitution itself, while it apparently did not contemplate the development of administrative relationships between the states and the central government, departed from federal theory in giving recognition, under certain conditions, to agreements and joint action by the states." [29] A statement made by the Technical Committee on Regional Planning of the National Resources Committee in 1935 indicates the cause of and, in a measure, justifies this departure: "There are interests and problems that do not coincide nicely either with the national boundaries or with State lines. Such interests may be badly served or not served at all by the ordinary channels of National or State political action." [30] It has been well said that "When a great river, with all its potentialities for both creation and destruction, sprawls through a community, it is easy to see . . . that the adequate harnessing of such a force both to meet competing demands for flood control, soil conservation, power production, irrigation, transportation, domestic and industrial use, and recreation and to fit it into a balanced and harmonious functioning of all the habitation, productive, and servicing components of the community will require the most careful calculation and integration of objectives for the whole area affected." [31] Segments of that area cannot afford either to plan or to act in isolation, if they would achieve their objectives. [32] Again, the Regional Planning Committee states: "Used earlier chiefly as an alternative to litigation before the Supreme Court . . . and hence of limited application, more recently the compacts and proposals for them reflect the emphasis on a positive provision for continuing and flexible adjustment of public services to needs that cannot be adequately met or dealt with at all by ordinary State or Federal action." [33] Yet, the measure of justification for the use of these "short circuits" is tied up with the degree of protection which the general requirement of congressional consent to such agreements affords the whole from injury through action of a combination formed by some of its component parts. Professor MacIver has well said, though in another connection, that "Government has the primary responsibility of safeguarding the whole against the part, and in our world of organized interests this responsibility has grown ever more comprehensive and more complicated."[34]

Increased economic interdependence and unity have made it necessary, in considering the advantages to be gleaned by the States parties to the agreement, to weigh those advantages against the possible disadvantages to be suffered in other regions in the resultant interaction. Donald Davidson asks, for example: Can TVA "relieve the economic disadvantage of the Tennessee Valley region (and in some measure of the upper South) without either doing harm to some distant region or changing to a marked degree the regional 'culture' which it is supposed to conserve?"[35] No one section can be treated in isolation from the others, for the interrelationships of the various sections of the country preclude such treatment without jeopardy to the interests of the remaining sections. Davidson continues: "As long as the supposedly 'national' economy is a sectional economy in disguise and remains exploitative in its action, the forces of political regionalism will jockey for power in the Federal Government, or, failing there, will endeavor to set up protective boundaries or their equivalent."[36] Again, "From many different branches of social study, surveying many different kinds of evidence, one conclusion emerges: sectionalism, or, if one prefers, regionalism, is a persistent and very likely an inherent condition of democratic government in the United States."[37] The compact's political, social, and economic repercussions may make it totally undesirable from the point of view of the whole, though quite desirable from the point of view of the region seeking its approval. As one student of the problem has pointed out, "only a static and very narrow conception of what constitutes the 'national interest' would hold that interstate and regional problems have no bearing on the welfare of the Nation as a whole. Without the necessity for Congressional consent, there would be no opportunity for considering such agreements in the light of broad public policy."[38]

The existence of sectional conflicts in American history cannot be denied. The Virginia and Kentucky Resolutions, the Hartford Convention, the War between the States, tariff legislation, and agricultural legislation, to indicate a few, bear witness and point to the fact that different sections have different interests, all of which must be considered in the light of the whole in the hope that through give and take the general interest may be achieved.[39]

The Supreme Court in the Maternity Act cases recognized the sectional issue involved in the grant-in-aid program, while dismissing the cases for want of jurisdiction: "It is . . . alleged that the burden of the appropriations provided by this act and similar legislation falls unequally upon the several states, and rests largely upon the industrial states. . . ."[40] The Court concluded, however, that the tax did not fall upon States but upon people. Invalidating the first "Triple A," the Court stated that the word "tax" was never "thought to connote the expropriation of money from one group for the benefit of another."[41] The powers of taxation and appropriation "extend only to matters of national, as distinguished from local, welfare."[42]

The lines cannot be sectional in a geographical sense alone, however, for the regionalists' ideas of "natural regions" and "regional homogeneity" break down in application. One commentator tersely advances the reason, stating: ". . . in spite of the regionalists' belief in the coincidence of areas of social phenomena, the Cotton Belt, the southern coal area, Atlanta's natural trading area, the Tennessee Valley, and the area of Charleston's social mores are not the same."[43] Thus, the TVA distributes electricity outside the Tennessee Valley. Not only does a watershed disregard state and national lines, but it also disregards those of other problem areas. For some purposes the South can be considered as a whole; for others it cannot. This is but to say that classification is dependent upon the criteria of the classifier. Also, discoveries of oil in Illinois, making that State one of the leaders in oil production, precipitated the question of whether it should not be a party to the Interstate Oil Compact.[44] What constitutes a "section" at one time, then, may not constitute one at a later time as a result of discoveries, developments, or change of some kind. Classification cannot be static. Too, a "section" may be based upon the presence of some resource and, thus, be constituted by the areas where those resources exist, although those areas are not contiguous. Sectionalism connotes conflict, but it is on the bases of conflict and cooperation that the general welfare will be achieved, if it is to be achieved. What is particularly necessary is that this conflict be so channeled or so limited as to prevent disruption of the whole. It is the role of Congress in granting or refusing its consent to see that this aim is achieved.

Mr. Ernest C. Carman in a recent article suggests amending the last paragraph of Section 10 in Article I of the Constitution to read: "No state shall, without the consent of Congress . . . enter into any agreement or compact with a foreign power. . . . All compacts and agreements between the States shall be subordinate to this Constitution and to all conflicting or inconsistent laws of Congress at any time enacted pursuant thereto; and no such compact shall cover any subject of national concern." [45] As the Federal Government is a government of delegated powers, and, presumably, all valid legislation would be enacted in pursuance to those powers, it would seem that the "Supremacy Clause" of the Constitution would render the subordination element of the revision superfluous. With the removal of the prior-consent requirement, the burden of decision as to whether a compact impinged upon "any subject of national concern" would rest upon the Supreme Court. In fact, Mr. Carman would amend Section 2 of Article III of the Constitution so as to give to the Supreme Court "original and exclusive jurisdiction in all matters or controversies arising from compacts or agreements between the States; including arbitral and declaratory relief and relief by advisory interpretation, which it shall be the duty of the court always to grant upon the petition of any interested State or of the United States." [46] Mr. Carman sees in this arrangement ample protection for the general public through exercise of the restraining power of the Supreme Court and through the congressional power to enact laws overriding and thus nullifying any compacts which might prove detrimental to the general interest. "By such amendment," he feels, moreover, "the balance between State and Federal power may be revised and set most definitely upon the principles of *locality* and *generality* which Abraham Lincoln conceived to be the guiding star for proper distribution of sovereignty between the States and the United States.

"And in this way the widely separated States of the far flung American Union will be permitted to adapt themselves to regional arrangements with their neighboring States, or to coordination of industrial or agricultural or other pursuits with more distant States having a common interest therein, but of such a nature that neither the remaining States nor the United States need have any concern therewith," [47] Mr. Carman adds.

This would be to substitute judicial review for prior congressional consent. It is asserted that use of the measures of "arbitral and declaratory relief and relief by advisory interpretation" would ameliorate or eliminate the evils of the usual "hit-and-miss' case treatment characteristic of judicial action. [48] Even if this were conceded, the proposal would remain subject to serious attack. Compacts would be judged by the single standard of legal philosophy and would not be considered in the light of national policy. Moreover, as Robert H. Jackson has pointed out, to the extent that the Supreme Court enforces its own views of good policy in performing its duty to enforce explicit constitutional provisions, in opposition to the majority, "it defeats government by representative democracy."[49] Certainly, shifting this policy area from the arena of Congress to the jurisdiction of the Court is equally a defeat for "government by representative democracy."

Yet, Professor Turner's prophecy to the effect that "the real federal aspect of our government will lie, not in the relation of state and nation, but in the relation of section and nation,"[50] has not been recognized in public law. It has been asserted that "deliberate exclusion of regions from all legal consideration has not, in the long run, resulted in a true Federalism, nor has it even preserved the interest of states. Instead it has brought about regional imperialism. That is, it has encouraged the appropriation of Federal authority by the region which has had the means to lay hold upon it, and it has reduced other regions (and within them the states) to the position of accomplices or servile dependents."[51] Proposals have been made, however, which, if put into effect, would realize this last element in Turner's prophecy.

One advocate of constitutional reform, branding his proposals "A Program for National Security," would erect "regional commonwealths" corresponding to the "persisting units of both cultural and economic values."[52] The States no longer constitute economic units and, for the most part, no longer possess "even as rough boundaries of cultural unity and traditional loyalties" sufficient vitality "to resist the inevitable march toward federal centralization."[53] The "regional commonwealths" would replace the States in the federal system and would be charged primarily with the responsibility for execution of federal laws, as the provinces are in Canada. This latter element would forestall concentration of our entire bureaucracy in Washington.[54] Yet, the States would be retained as administrative units comparable to the English counties. Presumably, the problem of coordination of the various levels of government would be simplified, as general policy would emanate from the top and filter down through the various governmental strata. The writer states that his plan "can, naturally enough, be dismissed wholesale with the dogmatic assertion that to talk of reorganizing our constitutional system along more rational lines is Utopian. The states are too firmly entrenched, one may assert, to be budged by constitutional methods from their vested legal rights. That may be."[55] And it probably is, for inertia is a potent factor. But he warns that "stand-pat conservatives" are always the ones who render the system's destruction inevitable in the crises of constitutional development by demanding the impossible of outmoded machinery.

"It is not those who would reform but those who would ossify a constitution who bring about its destruction. They are the true begetters of fascist Caesarism."[56] The latter is undoubtedly true, even to the point where it might be called a truism, but whether conditions have reached the stage where solution of supra-state, sub-national problems requires such drastic action as fundamental alteration of the whole constitutional system is certainly debatable. It is difficult to doubt the statement of Frankfurter and Landis that "The persistence of federalism in this country in substantially its present form, namely, as a Union of States is . . . an assured fact."[57] They maintain that "political and legal discussion" in order to be fruitful must accept continuance of that form of federalism for the immediate future "as a presupposition." That continuance in the eyes of Frankfurter and Landis is one "of the States approximately with their present legal autonomy, and not, like the departments of France, mere administrative divisions of the central government."[58]

All this serves merely to indicate an awareness of the existence of problem areas and sectional interests which pay little respect to state lines and which yet are sub-national in scope. Some means of coping with these problems and serving these interests is essential, it is granted. Also, it is to be noted that a federal system presents an added problem in the need to strike a balance which will preserve local initiative, participation, and responsibility and at the same time realize the national interest in optimum development of all its regions.[59] The Founding Fathers, in a somewhat negative fashion, it is true, made provision for one means in the Compact Clause of the Constitution.[60] It has been asserted that modern state legislatures confront problems whose stage is an interstate region for the resolution or handling of which "Collective legislative action through the instrumentality of compact by States constituting a region furnishes the answer."[61] Congressional legislation as to such regional problems in the nature of the situation would be ineffective. "Regional interests, regional wisdom and regional pride must be looked to for solutions."[62]

How Compacts Evolve. But what is the procedure by which these compacts have been, and are to be, evolved? No procedure was prescribed by the Constitution. Nor has Federal law filled the gap. Hence, the procedures followed in compact formulation have conformed to no single mold.[63] It has been stated that there are two methods of negotiating interstate compacts — the one by means of reciprocal legislation and the other by means of the "contract system."[64] In the former, a State enacts a law, thus tendering an offer, acceptance of which on the part of the other State or States involved is indicated by its or their enactment of the same law. The statute may provide for an exchange of formal ratification. Before this becomes a legal compact, however, it must receive congressional approval. The latter method, the contract system, is outlined by the National Resources Committee:

"There are five steps which must be, or may be, taken in negotiating and concluding an interstate compact; these are: (1) Congress authorizes the negotiation of the compact and outlines its purposes. (2) The State legislature authorizes commissioners representing them to meet and negotiate a compact. (3) The commissioners meet (under the chairmanship of a Federal representative) to negotiate and sign the compact. (4) The State legislatures ratify the compact. (5) Congress ratifies the compact."[65]

This was essentially the procedure employed in negotiation and ratification of the Colorado River compact. Arizona's protracted refusal to ratify the compact, however, resulted in the grant of congressional consent prior to the ratification by the legislatures of all the States concerned. Negotiation is carried on, as a rule, by commissions of the States authorized by the legislative or executive authorities to act on behalf of the States.[66] The contingent agreement which is produced as a result of their negotiation must be submitted to the respective state legislatures for approval.[67] A State may indicate its approval by legislative action in the form of a statutory offer to another State to be accepted by the latter's legislature, or by legislation paralleling that of the other State and embodying the agreement already reached by their representatives in negotiation of the compact. Ratification by the State is a legislative act, subject to veto by the governor.

As the subsequent step, Congress must grant its consent to the compact before it can go into effect. This congressional consent, however, may be granted in advance, granted subsequent to the ratification of the state legislatures, or, even in some cases, implied.[68] Congressional consent may be given by resolution or by statute and thus is subject to the veto power of the President. Congressional consent to the prison labor compact was given by executive order, the President acting under authority conferred upon him by the N. I. R. A.[69] Actually, the sole Federal function in connection with compacts between the States alone is the grant or refusal of congressional consent. However, the first step in the procedure outlined by the National Resources Committee may be included because of congressional desire to persuade action on the part of the States. This may be in the form of prior authorization or of a general invitation to the States or to some of them to enter a compact for a specific purpose. The principle of prior consent has been subjected to attack, however.

Franklin D. Roosevelt withheld approval of the Joint Resolution "to authorize compacts or agreements between or among the States bordering on the Atlantic Ocean with respect to fishing in the territorial waters and the bays and inlets of the Atlantic Ocean on which such States border . . .", stating: "This joint resolution is not in conformity with the usual and accepted method of granting the consent of the Congress to the execution of interstate compacts or agreements, in that it lacks a provision requiring the approval by the Congress of such compact or agreement as may be entered into before it shall become effective."[70] He continued: "I believe that it would be unwise to establish the policy of granting in advance the consent of the Congress to interstate compacts or agreements in connection with subjects described only in broad outline. . . ."[71]

Provision may be made, as in step 3 of the procedure outlined by the National Resources Committee, for a Federal representative on the negotiating commission as a result of congressional reluctance to relinquish participation in negotiations which interest it. Jane Perry Clark points to the fact that expansion of the Federal Government's sphere of action has enhanced the interest of that government in some of those subjects which the States have discovered they cannot handle without joint action on the part of several of their number. "Indeed, that increased federal interest," she observes, "makes it seem probable that the federal government will be increasingly discontented with the passive role of merely approving what states initate, or even with suggesting subjects on which the states may take action. Congress frequently wishes to keep its hand on the compacts of the states from the earliest to the last stages, particularly where such federal interests as navigable waterways are concerned."[72] Frequently, even after the compact's negotiation, legislation on the part of the respective States parties to it is necessary to make it effectual. Thus, in connection with a compact which establishes minimum standards, the signatory States must enact legislation embodying the standard requirements to which they have agreed.

What Compacts Contain. Most compacts would involve two States or a small group of States and would be designed for the local situation, differing with subject matter and "not a matter for uniformity."[73] While it is true that compacts are as diverse as their subject matter, they generally will contain roughly the same elements. As a rule, there will be sections indicating the legal basis of the compact, a statement of conditions which motivate consideration of the compact, the goals which the compact seeks to achieve, the obligation of the compact in terms of correlative rights and duties, definitions of terms as used in the compact, possibly a mode for the alteration of the compact, a statement of the time at which the compact takes effect, and the means by which the compact may be terminated or even a termination date. If the compact creates a commission or an authority, that organ may be granted merely the power to study methods, conditions, etc., and make recommendations, as in the case of the Interstate Oil Compact Commission, or it may be granted the authority to proceed with the regulation and development of the subject matter, as in the case of the Port of New York Authority with respect to the Port of New York. In lieu of the establishment of such a commission or authority, provision may be made whereby disagreements and problems arising later may be settled. Some compacts include a provision whereby the procedure permitting other States to become parties to the agreement is outlined. Thus, Article VIII of the Interstate Oil Compact provides that "Any oil producing state may become a party hereto by affixing its signature to a counterpart to be . . ." deposited in the archives of the Department of State of the United States and a duly certified copy to be forwarded to the governors of the signatory States and to be "ratified" by those States.

Inflexibility. It might be asserted that the compact device is entirely too inflexible to be of value in any but a limited application. In fact, it was stated in 1931 that "Experience up to date has been that" matters requiring cooperation to achieve uniformity "can best be handled by a uniform reciprocal act; but . . . similar and more binding results can be secured by a uniform interstate compact on the particular subject, in place of a uniform reciprocal act; and subjects may arise where the compact method is to be preferred."[74] It has also been said that the States, in restricting employment of "integrated contracts" during the early period of their history "to boundary disputes and partitions, exhibited a sensible awareness that, while there is a proper place for covenants and warranties even as between neighbors, true neighborliness rests on more flexible and more various expressions of good-will and helpfulness. The interstate compact is indeed the dignified senior of a large family of techniques and as such not to be disregarded; but the busy juniors are more numerous and more lively."[75] This points to a rigidity in the compact device which must be studied in the light of the use to which it is to be put.

A compact may be modified by a procedure similar to that of its negotiation, that is, through agreement between or among the States parties to the compact and consent to the change on the part of the general government. But such an amendment might well prove as difficult of attainment as negotiation of the original compact. Certainly such difficulty is incompatible with the emphasis indicated in the statement that "more recently the compacts and proposals for them reflect the emphasis on a positive provision for continuing and flexible adjustment of public services to needs that cannot be adequately met or dealt with at all by ordinary State or Federal action."[76] One commentator has stated that, "as an interstate agreement creates rights which may be altered only by consent of the parties, it is true that such an agreement is built more firmly into the legislative structure than unilateral or even reciprocal action on the part of the states concerned. Because of that fact, it is important at the time of negotiation for a state to be sure that it is not entering an agreement which might drag down its existing standards to the level of states with lower requirements."[77] The writer is concerned with compacts in their relation to social legislation, and, hence, the warning advanced is particularly necessary in the light of the need in such fields for constant adaptation of arrangements to changing conditions. There is a direct antithesis in emphasis between such compacts and those designed, for example, to settle boundary disputes, where the aim is finality. Provision for a termination date[78] or revision date can at least mitigate the possible evils of the ossified structure of which William Y. Elliott speaks.[79] Standards may be protected through a provision comparable to that in Title I of the minimum wage compact, wherein it was stated that "nothing herein contained shall be construed as abrogating, repealing, modifying or interfering with the operation of the laws already in effect in any State party hereto which establish standards equivalent to or above those herein specified, nor to prevent the enactment of additional laws establishing similar or higher standards; nor shall anything herein contained repeal or affect any laws concerning conditions of employment that are not in conflict herewith or that deal with subjects not included herein."[80] Also, it has been pointed out that "For practical purposes flexibility in statutory provisions enacted in pursuance of a compact is of equal importance with the possibility of amending the agreement itself."[81] Failure to provide some means for development, revision, and continuing adjustment may well mean that the compact contains the seeds of its own destruction.

[1] Some commentators indicate a third method of settling disputes between States in the legislative power of Congress. But this method is restricted to the

delegated powers and cannot be comprehensive in its scope. See William J. Donovan, "State Compacts As A Method of Settling Problems Common to Several States." *University of Pennsylvania Law Review,* 80:5, November, 1931, and "Interstate Compacts As A Means of Settling Disputes between States." *Harvard Law Review,* 35:322, January, 1922.

[2] James Brown Scott, "The Role of the Supreme Court of the United States in the Settlement of Interstate Disputes." *Selected Essays on Constitutional Law* (5 vols.; Chicago: The Foundation Press, 1938), III, 1541.

[3] Charles M. Andrews, *The Colonial Period of American History* (New Haven: Yale University Press, 1934), II, 54, 51; William Henry Fry, *New Hampshire As A Royal Province* (New York: Columbia University, 1908), p. 263. In connection with the Massachusetts-New Hampshire controversy, Governor Jonathan Belcher wrote a letter to the Board of Trade, saying: "The poor borderers on the lines . . . live like toads under the harrow, being run into jails on the one side or the other as often as they please to quarrel. They will pull down one another's houses, often wound one another and I fear it will end in bloodshed, unless his Majesty . . . give some effectual order to have the bounds fixed. . . . I now do not, nor do I ever, expect to see it settled but by a peremptory order from his Majesty, appointing commissioners to do it." Fry, *op. cit.,* p. 249. As to the effect of the issuance of an explanatory charter to Massachusetts upon Connecticut's yielding on the boundary issue and leaving the decision to the King, see Andrews, *op. cit.,* IV, 392-93. The case of *The Colony of Rhode Island* v. *The Colony of Connecticut* is to be found in James Brown Scott, editor, *Judicial Settlement of Controversies between States of the American Union* (New York: Oxford University Press, 1918), I, 573-76, and that of *The Colony of Rhode Island* v. *The Colony of Massachusetts* in *ibid.,* pp. 577-85. The case of *Penn* v. *Lord Baltimore,* a suit filed in 1735 between the proprietors of provinces granted by the Crown, to settle boundaries, is also treated in *ibid.,* pp. 585-600. A list of nine intercolonial agreements is to be found in Felix Frankfurter and J. M. Landis, "The Compact Clause of the Constitution – A Study in Interstate Adjustments." *Yale Law Journal,* 34:730-32, May, 1925, where the legislative, judicial, and administrative history of intercolonial and interstate compacts is given.

[4] *Articles of Confederation,* Article IX. [5] *Ibid.*

[6] Charles Warren, "The Supreme Court and Disputes between States." *Bulletin of the College of William and Mary,* 34:9, June, 1940. Frankfurter and Landis, *op. cit.,* pp. 732-34, list four interstate compacts under the Articles of Confederation.

[7] *Articles of Confederation,* Article VI.

[8] Joseph Story, *Commentaries on the Constitution of the United States* (3rd edition; Boston: Little, Brown and Company, 1858), II, 309, footnote 2.

[9] Max Farrand, editor, *The Records of the Federal Convention of 1787* (New Haven: Yale University Press, 1911), I, 316-17.

[10] *Ibid.,* p. 317. The report of the point as reproduced in Farrand's *Records* runs as follows: "He observed that the plan of Mr. Pat-son besides omitting a controul over the States as a general defence of the federal prerogatives was particularly defective in two of its provisions. 1. Its ratification was not to be by the people at large, but by the *Legislatures.* It could not therefore render the acts of Congs. in pursuance of their powers even legally *paramount* to the Acts of the States. 2. It gave (to the federal tribunal) an appellate jurisdiction only—even in the criminal cases enumerated, The necessity of any such provision supposed a

danger of undue acquittals in the State tribunals. Of what avail wd. an appellate tribunal be, after an acquttal? Besides in most if not all of the States, the Executives have by their respective *Constitutions* the right of pardg. How could this be taken from them by a *legislative* ratification only?" It is worthy of remark that the Patterson Plan presupposed continuance of the system established by the Articles of Confederation, being designed to render those Articles "so revised, corrected, & enlarged as to render the federal Constitution adequate to the Exigencies of Government, & the Preservation of the Union." *Ibid.*, III, 612, Appendix E. As already noted, Article IX of the Articles made provision for the settlement of "disputes and differences . . . subsisting . . . between two or more states . . ." See *supra*, p. 2. Madison himself reports the Patterson resolutions: "Resd. that in addition to the powers vested in the U. States in Congress, by the present existing articles of Confederation, they be authorized to . . ." and proceeds to indicate the additional powers. *Ibid.*, I, 243. Madison also records as follows the section resolving "that a federal Judiciary be established to consist of a supreme Tribunal . . .; that the Judiciary . . . shall have authority to hear and determine in the first instance on all impeachments of federal officers, & by way of appeal in the dernier resort . . . in all cases in which foreigners may be interested, in the construction of any treaty or treaties or which may arise on any of the Acts for regulation of trade, or the collection of the federal Revenue. . . ." *Ibid.*, p. 244. Quite apparently, then, Madison was aware of the fact that the Supreme Court was granted original jurisdiction in some cases by the Patterson Plan, but felt the grant inadequate.

[12] *Ibid.*, II, 160-63, 170-71, 172-73 183-85, 186, 396, 400-401.

[13] *Ibid.*, p. 401. [14] *Ibid.*

[15] Cognizant of the fact that the power was provided in the final arrangement, a critic, Luther Martin, speaking before the Maryland House of Representatives, stated that, if the powers of the federal "Judiciaries" were incompetent to carry into execution the "extensive plan" projected as to their jurisdiction in the Constitution, "other, and more certain Engines of power are supplied by the standing Army – unlimited as to number or its duration, in addition to [which] this Government has the entire Command of the Militia. . . ." *Ibid.*, III, 157. Martin was speaking here of the enforcement of federal law generally, however, rather than of decrees in controversies between states specifically. His observation is noteworthy as an indication of an awareness that the decrees of the federal judiciary were to be backed by the strong arm of the Federal Government.

[16] *Constitution of the United States,* Article III, section 2. Ezra Stiles wrote in his Diary: "They were unanimous . . . in the Expedy & Necessy of a supreme judiciary Tribunal of universal Jurisdiction – In Controversies of a legal Nature between States. . . ." As quoted in Farrand, *op. cit.*, III, 169. This development may be followed in Farrand, *op. cit.*, I, 211, 220, 223-24, 232, 237, 238; II, 39, 46, 132-33, 136, 146-47, 160-63, 170-71, 172-73, 183-86, 396, 400-401, 432, 576, 600.

Mr. Justice Bradley remarked in *Hans* v. *Louisiana,* 134 U.S. 1, 15 (1890), that the Constitution made some things "justiciable which were not known as such at the common law; such, for example, as controversies between States as to boundary lines, and other questions admitting of judicial solution. . . . The establishment of this new branch of jurisdiction seemed to be necessary from the extinguishment of diplomatic relations between the States." The significance of the jurisdiction granted to the Court in "controversies between two or more States" was indicated in 1887, when the Constitution was almost a century old, by the Court's list of such cases in *Wisconsin* v. *Pelican Ins. Co.*, 127 U.S. 265, 288 (1888): "The most numerous class of which this court has entertained jurisdiction is that of controversies between two States as to the boundaries of their territory, such as were determined before the Revolution by the King in Council, and under the Articles of Confederation (while there was no national judiciary) by committees or commissioners appointed by Congress. . . . *New Jersey* v. *New York*, 3 Pet. 461; 5 Pet. 283; 6 Pet. 323; *Rhode Island* v. *Massachusetts*, 12 Pet. 657, 724, 736, 759; 13 Pet. 23; 14 Pet. 210; 15 Pet. 233; 4 How. 591, 628; *Missouri* v. *Iowa*, 7 How. 660, and 10 How. 1; *Florida* v. *Georgia*, 17 How. 478; *Alabama* v. *Georgia*, 23 How. 505; *Virginia* v. *West Virginia*, 11 Wall. 39; *Missouri* v. *Kentucky*, 11 Wall. 395. See also *Georgia* v. *Stanton*, 6 Wall. 50, 72, 73."

[17] Scott, "The Role of the Supreme Court of the United States in the Settlement of Interstate Disputes," p. 1542.

[18] Charles Warren, *The Supreme Court and Sovereign States* (Princeton, N. J.: Princeton University Press, 1924), p. 68.

[19] See *Washington* v. *Oregon*, 214 U.S. 205, 217-18 (1909); *Minnesota* v. *Wisconsin*, 252 U.S. 273, 283 (1920); and *New York* v. *New Jersey*, 256 U.S. 296, 313 (1921).

[20] Farrand, *op. cit.*, III, 548. This quotation is taken from a section entitled, "James Madison: Preface to Debates in the Convention of 1787."

[21] *Ibid.*, p. 549.

[22] Madison, however, in another connection, after citing the intrigues practiced in the historical confederacies by foreign powers, pointed out that "The plan of Mr. Patterson, not giving to the general Councils any negative on the will of the particular States, left the door open for the like pernicious machinations among ourselves." Farrand, *op. cit.*, I, 319. This statement was advanced in consideration of the question: "Will it secure the Union agst. the influence of foreign powers over its members." Also, "He pretended not to say that any such influence had yet been tried: but it [is] naturally to be expected that occasions would produce it." *Ibid.*

[23] See *Ibid.*, II, 625-26, 633-34, 169, 187, 577, 597.

[24] Charles Warren, *The Making of the Constitution* (Boston: Little, Brown and Company, 1937), p. 550.

[25] Clause 1 of Section 10 provides that "No State shall enter into any Treaty, Alliance, or Confederation . . ." See *infra*, Ch. II, for distinction in public law between "treaties" and "compacts."

[26] *The Federalist* (New York: The Heritage Press, 1945), p. 300.

[27] See Jonathan Elliot, editor, *The Debates in the Several State Conventions on the Adoption of the Federal Constitution, As Recommended by the General Convention at Philadelphia, in 1787* (2d edition; Philadelphia: J. B. Lippincott Company, 1901).

[28] Frankfurter and Landis, *op. cit.*, p. 694.

[29] Garland C. Routt, "Interstate Compacts and Administrative Co-operation." *The Annals of the American Academy of Political and Social Science*, 207:93, January, 1940.

[30] National Resources Committee, *Regional Factors in National Planning and Development* (Washington: U.S. Government Printing Office, 1935), p. 34.

[31] Myres S. McDougal, "Regional Planning and Development: The Process of Using Intelligence under Conditions of Resource and Institutional Interdependence for Securing Community Values." *Iowa Law Review*, 32:197, January, 1947.

[32] "It is . . . certain very definite interdependences, such as those created by a great river system, in the conditions under which a community must seek its objectives that make necessary the introducing into the planning process of certain areal, including *regional* perspectives." *Ibid.*

[33] National Resources Committee, *op. cit.*, p. 36.

[34] R. M. MacIver, *The Web of Government* (New York: The Macmillan Company, 1947), p. 350. MacIver was concerned with the "conflicts of opposing interests" as focused in the "clashes of opposing organizations" and the role of government in connection therewith. Swisher sees a new type of federalism in which there are to be found below the Federal Government "not only the states but also, and often on lines roughly parallel with the states, the more powerful corporations of the country, with labor unions in some instances not much lower than the same parallel lines." These corporations, he points out, differ from the States in their power to combine as well as engage in business strife, while "The Constitution forbids the states to make compacts with one another without the consent of Congress, and two or more states may not merge into a single state without congressional authorization." According to this view the States are at a comparative disadvantage, and it may well be that the government's responsibility for safeguarding the whole will prove more onerous in execution in connection with the new federalism than with the old. Carl Brent Swisher, *The Growth of Constitutional Power in the United States* (Chicago: The University of Chicago Press, 1946), pp. 238, 239.

[35] Donald Davidson, "Political Regionalism and Administrative Regionalism." *The Annals of the American Academy of Political and Social Science*, 207: 141, January, 1940.

[36] *Ibid.*, p. 143. An indication of how deeply Mr. Davidson feels on this matter is given by his statement: "Suffice it to say that rebellious regions like the South and the West would be less rebellious if they could not accuse the Federal Government of subsidizing and protecting the economy which despoils them, while at the same time it frustrates their own efforts at self-protection and thus deprives them of all recourse." This would indicate that the present balance of interests is an unjust one, but even in its assertion of injustice it points to the existence of competitive regions and the determining influence of the general government in the adjustment of their relations.

[37] Donald Davidson, *The Attack on Leviathan: Regionalism and Nationalism in the United States* (Chapel Hill: The University of North Carolina Press, 1938), p. 102.

[38] Routt, *op. cit.*, p. 100.

[39] For an exceedingly apt forecast of some twenty years back of the part to be played by sections in the history of the United States, see Frederick J. Turner, *The Significance of Sections in American History* (New York: Henry Holt and Company, 1932), pp. 313-14. ". . . as the nation reaches a more stable equilibrium, a more settled state of society, with denser populations pressing upon the means of existence, with this population no longer migratory, the influence of the diverse physiographic provinces which make up the nation will become more marked. They will exercise sectionalizing influences, tending to mould society to their separate conditions, in spite of all the countervailing tendencies toward

national uniformity. National action will be forced to recognize and adjust itself to these conflicting sectional interests. The more the nation is organized on the principle of direct majority rule, and consolidation, the more sectional resistance is likely to manifest itself. Statesmen in the future, as in the past, will achieve their leadership by voicing the interests and ideas of the sections which have shaped these leaders, and they will exert their influence nationally by making combinations between sections and by accommodating their policy to the needs of such alliances. Congressional legislation will be shaped by compromises and combinations, which will in effect be treaties between rival sections, and the real federal aspect of our government will lie, not in the relation of state and nation, but in the relation of section and nation." See also Elwyn A. Mauck, "Interregional Relations." *The Annals of the American Academy of Political and Social Science,* 207: 124-29, January, 1940.

[40] *Massachusetts* v. *Mellon; Frothingham* v. *Mellon,* 262 U.S. 447, 479 (1923).

[41] *United States v. Butler,* 297 U.S. 1, 61 (1936). [42] *Ibid.,* p. 67.

[43] James W. Fesler, "Federal Use of Administrative Areas." *The Annals of the American Academy of Political and Social Science,* 207:111, January, 1940. See also James W. Fesler, "Standardization of Federal Administrative Regions." *Social Forces,* 15:12-21, October, 1936.

[44] See Hubert R. Gallagher, "Work of the Commissions on Interstate Cooperation." *The Annals of the American Academy of Political and Social Science,* 207: 107, January, 1940.

[45] Ernest C. Carman, "Should the States Be Permitted to Make Compacts without the Consent of Congress?" *Cornell Law Quarterly,* 23:283, February, 1938.

[46] *Ibid.,* p. 284.

[47] *Ibid.* Lincoln's concept of "locality and generality" was expressed in his message of July 4, 1861, to a special session of Congress. "This relative matter of national power and State rights, as a principle, is no other than the principle of *generality* and *locality.* Whatever concerns the whole should be confided to the whole — to the General Government— while whatever concerns *only* the State should be left exclusively to the State. This is all there is of original principle about it." James D. Richardson, editor, *A Compilation of the Messages and Papers of the Presidents* (New York: Bureau of National Literature, 1897), VIII, 3229.

[48] It is this inherent weakness in the judicial approach to such matters which has led to the suggestion that they might be treated more comprehensively and, hence, more advantageously by Congress than by the Court. Thus, Mr. Justice Black has counseled restraint on the part of the Court in connection with state activities relative to interstate commerce in order that Congress may attack the problem in the comprehensive way of which it alone is capable. "Judicial control of national commerce — unlike legislative regulations — must from inherent limitations of the judicial process treat the subject by the hit and miss method of deciding single local controversies upon evidence and information limited by the narrow rules of litigation. Spasmodic and unrelated instances of litigation cannot afford an adequate basis for the creation of integrated national rules which alone can afford that full protection for interstate commerce intended by the Constitution. We would, therefore, leave the questions raised . . . for consideration of Congress in a nation-wide survey of the constantly increasing barriers to trade among the states. Unconfined by 'the narrow scope of judicial proceedings' Congress alone can, in the exercise of its plenary control over interstate commerce,

. . . on the basis of full exploration of the many aspects of a complicated problem devise a national policy fair alike to the states and our Union. Diverse and interacting state laws may well have created avoidable hardships. . . . But the remedy, if any is called for, we think is within the ample reach of Congress." *McCarroll* v. *Dixie Greyhound Lines, Inc.*, 309 U.S. 176, 189 (1940).

[49] Robert H. Jackson, *The Struggle for Judicial Supremacy* (New York: Alfred A. Knopf, 1941), p. 316. Mr. Jackson has two chapters on "Government by Lawsuit" and "The Political Nature of Judicial Supremacy" which might well be read in this connection. *Ibid.*, pp. 286-327.

[50] Turner, *op. cit.*, p. 314. *See supra,* footnote 39.

[51] Davidson, *The Attack on Leviathan,* p. 111. Davidson states that "The vicious element is not regionalism but regional imperialism." *Ibid.*, p. 117.

[52] William Y. Elliott, *The Need for Constitutional Reform* (New York: McGraw-Hill Book Company, 1935), p. 193. This is an exceedingly provocative study upon the proposals of which one might well pause to reflect.

[53] *Ibid.*, p. 191. [54] *Ibid.*, p. 193.

[55] *Ibid.*, p. 205. [56] *Ibid.*, pp. 207-208.

[57] Frankfurter and Landis, *op. cit.*, p. 687. [58] *Ibid.*

[59] McDougal, *op. cit.*, p. 200.

[60] It may well be that the Founding Fathers did not contemplate in their provisions the uses to which the Compact Clause has been, and is being put. See *infra,* Ch. V. Frankfurter and Landis state that "The Constitution puts this power negatively in order to express the limitation imposed upon its exercise. By putting this authority for State action in a section dealing with restrictions upon the States, the significance of what was granted has probably been considerably minimized." Frankfurter and Landis, *op. cit.*, p. 691, footnote 25.

[61] *Ibid.*, p. 708. [62] *Ibid.*

[63] The Committee on Uniform Act for Compacts and Agreements between States in its Report to the National Conference of Commissioners on Uniform State Laws in 1931, indeed, stated that "in view of the importance of interstate compacts and their value in many ways, the Conference could consider whether it would wish to propose a uniform procedure for framing compacts that would simplify the process and make it easier for states to enter into them." *Handbook of the National Conference of Commissioners on Uniform State Laws* (Baltimore, Md.: The Lord Baltimore Press, 1931), p. 360. In 1935 the Conference authorized creation of a State Commission on Interstate Cooperation, which, among other things, was "to promote and expedite the use of the provision of the Constitution of the United States permitting negotiation of Compacts and Agreements among the states." *Handbook of the National Conference of Commissioners on Uniform State Laws* (1935), p. 88. Then, in 1936, it so amended its constitution, changing the scope of its activities, as to enable it to sponsor "model laws on (a) subjects suitable for interstate compacts, and (b) subjects in which uniformity will make more effective the exercise of state powers and promote interstate cooperation. . . ." *Handbook of the National Conference of Commissioners on Uniform State Laws* (1936), p. 118.

[64] Alice M. Dodd, "Interstate Compacts." *United States Law Review,* 70:558, October, 1936.

[65] National Resources Committee, *op. cit.*, p. 53.

[66] Practical considerations usually point to the preferability of legislative au-

thorization, if for no other reason than the financial provision for expenses.

[67] It is possible to eliminate the necessity for ratification by the state legislatures through provision that the compact when negotiated by the commissioners will become obligatory for the States participating. Thus, the statutes authorizing establishment of the Port of New York Authority provide that the compact "when signed and sealed by the commissioners of each state as hereinbefore provided, and the attorney-general of the state of New York, and the attorney-general of the state of New Jersey if he be designated so to act by the state of New Jersey, shall become binding upon the state of New York, and shall be filed in the office of the secretary of state of the state of New York." *Laws of New York, 1921,* Ch. 154, art. XXII, sec. 2. See also *Laws of New Jersey, 1921,* Ch. 151, art. XXII, sec. 2; 42 United States *Statutes at Large* 174, Ch. 77. In the 1931 Report of Committee on Uniform Act for Compacts and Agreements between States to the National Conference of Commissioners on Uniform State Laws, it was suggested: "Granted that interstate compacts are desirable, . . . the Conference might make their formation easier than it now is. At present, to form such a compact, each state by its legislature passes a resolution or act providing for a commission or committee to negotiate with the other states, and when this is accomplished, the commission reports back to the legislature to have the compact approved. At least two sessions of the legislature are required. It would be much simpler to provide, by a uniform constitutional amendment to be recommended to all the states by the Conference, that the Governor shall have power, by and with the advice and consent of the Senate, to make compacts and agreements with other states and foreign governments. This would follow the provisions of the United States Constitution giving the President treaty-making power. Of course the consent of Congress must be obtained under the United States Constitution to interstate compacts." *Handbook of the National Conference of Commissioners on Uniform State Laws* (1931), pp. 360-61.

[68] See *infra,* Ch. III, for treatment of this matter of congressional consent in respect to public law.

[69] Jane P. Clark, "Interstate Compacts and Social Legislation I." *Political Science Quarterly,* 50:524, December, 1935.

[70] *Congressional Record,* Vol. 84, pt. 10, p. 11175, August 5, 1939. Also it has been stated that: "The framing of a Congressional act giving consent in advance to the formation of state compacts dealing with specific subjects is objectionable upon several grounds. The first is that your committee does not know these concrete subjects in which compacts suggest themselves as the desirable arrangement. The compact by its very nature being a regional matter is put beyond the concern of this Conference. . . . If, on the other hand, all that is asked is the framing of legislation whereby Congress should give its consent to states forming compacts generally upon such matters as river apportionment, harbor regulation, forestry regulation, and the like, such legislation seems objectionable because it requires Congress to give its assent to very indefinite propositions. Such legislation has no practical value from the standpoint of inducing states to act. It is responsive to nothing more than a mere academic urge and reflects no concrete aim of the states." *Report of the Committee on Interstate Compacts of the Conference on Uniform State Laws, 1931,* pp. 30-31.

[71] *Congressional Record,* Vol. 84, pt. 10, p. 11175, August 5, 1939.

[72] Jane P. Clark, *The Rise of a New Federalism: Federal-State Cooperation in the United States* (New York: Columbia University Press, 1938), p. 72.

[73] *Handbook of the National Conference of Commissioners on Uniform State Laws* (1931), p. 360.

[74] *Ibid.*

[75] Albert S. Abel, "Interstate Cooperation As A Child." *Iowa Law Review*, 32:206, January, 1947.

[76] National Resources Committee, *op. cit.*, p. 36.

[77] Jane P. Clark, "Interstate Compacts and Social Legislation II." *Political Science Quarterly*, 51:36, March, 1936.

[78] This was the arrangement made by the Interstate Oil Compact of 1935, Article VIII of which stated: "This compact shall expire September 1, 1937. But any state joining herein may, upon sixty days' notice, withdraw herefrom."

[79] See *supra*, pp. 9-10. This consideration bolstered the belief of Thomas Jefferson that each generation should give to itself the fundamental law under which it was to live, leading him to favor constitutional conventions every nineteen years. See Paul L. Ford, editor, *The Writings of Thomas Jefferson* (New York and London: G. P. Putnam's Sons, 1892-1899), V, 121-24; X, 42-44.

[80] *Minimum Wage Compact*, Title I.

[81] Clark, "Interstate Compacts and Social Legislation II," p. 37.

Chapter II

THE COURT LOOKS AT THE MEANING OF THE COMPACT CLAUSE

What are the precise meanings of the terms "agreement" and "compact" as these terms are used in the constitutional prohibition expressed in Clause 3 of Section 10 of Article I: "No State shall, without the consent of Congress, . . . enter into any agreement or compact with another State or with a foreign power. . . ."? Clause 1 of the same section states that "No State shall enter into any Treaty, Alliance, or Confederation. . . ." The prohibition is absolute. Wherein does the difference lie between a "Treaty, Alliance, or Confederation," absolutely prohibited, and an "agreement or compact," prohibited only if that agreement or compact is not sanctioned by Congress?

Treaties and Compacts Distinguished. What did the terms "treaty" and "compact" mean to the Framers of the Constitution? As one writer has pointed out, "The fact that the draftsmen of the Articles of Confederation while working on three different drafts in the period of one and one-half years consistently gave the States a limited right to enter into agreements with foreign powers, and gave them an unlimited[1] right to enter into agreements among themselves and the further fact that ten years later, in the Constitution, the rights of the States to enter into agreements among themselves became limited, show that the men of those times used 'agreement' as if the word had a distinct and clear meaning for them and not merely as a catch-all term to supplement others."[2] It would seem self-evident from the inclusion of the two provisions relative to treaties and compacts in the Constitution, the one of which would form a contradiction to the other if the terms were synonomous, that the Framers did distinguish them in meaning. At any rate, the fact that the Framers, many of them trained lawyers who would be acutely aware of the extreme importance of word-meanings in such a document, had these clauses before them for a considerable period and approved them without question justifies the conclusion that "The only reasonable explanation of this phenomenon is that the words 'agreements or compacts' in contrast to 'treaties' were used as technical terms taken from the field of international dealings, that they were words of art, carried a definite meaning and therefore called for no discussion."[3]

Of the works with which the Framers were familiar on "international dealings," those of Hugo Grotius and Emmerich de Vattel made such distinctions.[4] Grotius differentiated treaties (*federa*) from other agreements (*pactiones aliae*), but, as has been observed, the definitions given to those terms by Grotius "could not possibly [have] be[en] relied upon by the framers of the constitution because of the remoteness of the subject matter embraced in the definitions."[5] Grotius stated that "public conventions," which he defined as "those which cannot be made but by the authority and in the name of the sovereign power . . .,"[6] distinguishing them from the private contracts of individuals and the personal contracts of the sovereigns, "may be divided into treaties, engagements, and other compacts."[7] Drawing from Livy, he defined treaties as "those contracts, which are made by the express authority of the sovereign power, and in which the people invoke the divine vengeance on their heads, if they violate their engagements." An engagement "is what was made by persons, who had no express commission for that purpose from the sovereign power, and whose acts consequently required a further ratification from the sovereign himself."[8] The "other compacts" he left for his readers' definition, except to indicate that they, or part of them, form a subdivision of "public conventions."

Vattel was more helpful in advancing the following definitions:

"Section 152. Treaties of Alliance and other public treaties . . . . . A treaty, in Latin *foedus,* is a pact entered into by sovereigns for the welfare of the State, either in perpetuity or for a considerable length of time.

"Sec. 153. Compacts, agreements or conventions. Pacts which have for their object matters of temporary interest are called agreements, conventions, compacts. They are fulfilled by a single act and not by a continuous performance of acts. When the act in question is performed these pacts are executed once and for all; whereas treaties are executory in character and the acts called for must continue as long as the treaty exists.

"Sec. 192. Treaties executed by an act done once for all. Treaties which do not call for continuous acts, but are fulfilled by a single act, and are thus executed once for all, those treaties, unless indeed we prefer to give them another name, (see Sec. 153), those conventions, those pacts which are executed by an act done once for all and not by successive acts, are, when once carried out, fully and definitely consummated. If valid, they naturally bring about a permanent and irrevocable state of things. . . ."[9]

Mr. Weinfeld contends — and very convincingly — that the "agreement or compact" of the Constitution is the same as Vattel's "agreement, convention, compact" ("accord, convention, paction") in sections 153 and 192.[10] He is led, by a study of Vattel's definitions of terms and by an expansion of the term "agreements or compacts" so that it would "include the 'agreements' and the 'compact' . . . as entered into between various states under the Articles of Confederation," to conclude that "agreements or compacts' as intended by the framers of the Constitution included (1) settlements of boundary lines with attending cession or exchange of strips of land, (2) regulation of matters connected with boundaries as for instance regulation of jurisdiction of offenses committed on boundary waters, of fisheries or of navigation."[11] Be that as it may, "we must never forget," as Chief Justice Marshall once said, "that it is a *constitution* we are expounding,"[12] and the Court has heeded this admonition. Hence the compact device has been employed for other than these uses, and the Court has sustained the employment.[13]

No less an authority than Joseph Story observes, with respect to the two provisions involving "treaties" and "compacts," that "Perhaps the language of the former clause may be more plausibly interpreted from the terms used, 'treaty, alliance, or confederation,' and upon the ground, that the sense of each is best known by its association (*noscitur a sociis*) to apply to treaties of a political character; such as treaties of alliance for purposes of peace and war; and treaties of confederation in which the parties are leagued for mutual government, political cooperation, and the exercise of political sovereignty; and treaties of cession of sovereignty, or conferring internal political jurisdiction, or external political dependence, or general commercial privileges. The latter clause, 'compacts and agreements,' might then very properly apply to such as regarded what might be deemed mere private rights of sovereignty; such as questions of boundary; interests in land situated in the territory of each other; and other internal regulations for the mutual comfort and convenience of states, bordering on each other."[14] In such cases "the consent of congress may be properly required, in order to check any infringement of the rights of the national government; and at the same time a total prohibition to enter into any compact or agreement, might be attended with permanent inconvenience, or public mischief."[15]

What constitutes an "agreement" or "compact" was considered in *Virginia* v. *Tennessee*, where the Supreme Court sustained the Virginia-Tennessee compact of 1803 establishing what the Court held to be the real, certain, and true boundary between the States[16] and denied the prayer of Virginia to have the compact set aside and annulled and a new boundary line run. The Court stated that compacts or agreements cover "all stipulations affecting the conduct or claims of the parties."[17] The Virginia-Tennessee compact, then, was one within the meaning of the Compact Clause and required congressional approval for its validity. That approval was fairly to be implied from subsequent congressional legislation and proceedings upon the compact treating the line established as the true boundary.[18] In this case, the Court, considering what constitutes an "agreement or compact," stated that "The terms 'agreement' or 'compact' taken by themselves are sufficiently comprehensive to embrace all forms of stipulation, written or verbal, and relating to all kinds of subjects; to those to which the United States can have no possible objection or have any interest in interfering with, as well as to those which may tend to increase and build up the political influence of the contracting States, so as to encroach upon or impair the supremacy of the United States or interfere with their rightful management of particular subjects placed under their entire control."[19] Since the Court indicated that there were many matters upon which different States might agree that could in no respect concern the United States, however, it is reasonable to infer that such items do not constitute interstate "agreements or compacts" within the meaning of the constitutional provision requiring congressional approval. The following were listed as examples.

"If, for instance, Virginia should come into possession and ownership of a small parcel of land in New York which the latter State might desire to acquire as a site for a public building, it would hardly be deemed essential for the latter State to obtain the consent of Congress before it could make a valid agreement with Virginia for the purchase of the land. If Massachusetts, in forwarding its exhibits to the Worlds Fair at Chicago, should desire to transport them a part of the distance over the Erie Canal, it would hardly be deemed essential for that State to obtain the consent of Congress before it could contract with New York for the transportation of the exhibits through that State in that way. If the bordering line of two States should cross some malarious and disease-producing district, there could be no possible reason, on any conceivable public grounds, to obtain the consent of Congress for the bordering States to agree to unite in draining the district, and thus removing the cause of disease. So in case of threatened invasion of cholera, plague, or other causes of sickness and death, it would be the height of absurdity to hold that the threatened States could not unite in providing means to prevent and repel the invasion of the pestilence, without obtaining the consent of Congress, which might not be at the time in session."[20]

If, then, the terms "compact" or "agreement" in the Constitution do not apply to every possible compact or agreement between one State and another, for the validity of which the consent of Congress must be obtained, to what compacts or agreements does the Constitution apply? Looking at the object of the constitutional provision and construing the terms agreement and compact by reference to it, the Court points out that "it is evident that the prohibition is directed to the formation of any combination tending to the increase of political power in the States, which may encroach upon or interfere with the just supremacy of the United States."[21] The Court proceeded, then, to quote with approval the observations of Story already noted[22] as to the distinction between "treaties," on the one hand, and "agreements or compacts" on the other. But this distinction has not always been so clear in court opinions.

Some indication of the distinction between "Treaties, Alliances, or Confederations," on the one hand, and "agreements or compacts," on the other, is afforded by the ruling of the Court in *Williams* v. *Bruffy*,[23] where a Confederate sequestration act was treated as a law of the State in which it was enforced and was invalidated as an impairment of the obligation of contracts. The reason for the Court's treating the sequestration act as a law of the State where it was enforced was made manifest by the Court's holding that there was "no validity in any legislation of the Confederate States"[24] which the Court could recognize, the Court distinguishing that body from the States which composed it. This holding was on the ground that the Constitution of the United States prohibits any treaty, alliance, or confederation by one State with another.[25] Hence, the organization called the Confederate States of America could not be regarded by the Court as having any legal existence.[26] This, then, is a confederation within the meaning of the absolute prohibition thereof in the Constitution.

In the case of *Holmes* v. *Jennison*,[27] moreover, the Court considered the validity of a State's exercise of the power to surrender fugitives from justice to another nation, in this case, Canada. A majority of the Court concurred in the opinion that the Governor of Vermont lacked the power to deliver up to a foreign government a person charged with having committed a crime in the territory of that government. But upon the question of jurisdiction the Court was equally divided. Five opinions were rendered by the eight Justices who sat on the case. Chief Justice Taney, speaking for himself and three of his colleagues, pointed out that the power to surrender fugitives to another nation is "a part of the foreign intercourse" of the country included within the treaty-making power. The power to make treaties is given by the Constitution in general terms, without any description of the objects intended to fall within its purview, and, consequently, it was designed to include all those subjects, which in the ordinary intercourse of nations were usually made subjects of negotiation and treaty and which were consistent with the nature of our institutions and the distribution of powers between the general and state governments.[28] But is the power to make treaties exclusive? It is evident that the general government possesses the power in question; it remains to inquire whether it has been surrendered by the States.[29] Taney answered this inquiry in the affirmative upon two grounds. According to the express words of the Constitution, it is one of the powers which the State may not exercise without congressional consent, and its exercise by the States is incompatible and inconsistent with the powers conferred on the Federal Government.[30] The Chief Justice apparently confused his reasoning here. He indicated that the power to surrender fugitives to another nation was "a part of the foreign intercourse" of the country included within the treaty-making power, the exercise of which was to be by "treaty." Thus its exercise by the States falls within the absolute prohibition of the Constitution. Yet Chief Justice Taney proceeded to treat it as "one of the powers that the states are forbidden to exercise without the consent of Congress." Even the consent of Congress cannot sanction a State's entry into a "treaty." These words are applicable only to an "agreement or compact," and the Chief Justice so recognized. But by terming the rendition arrangement a part of the foreign intercourse of the country included within the treaty-making power and then treating it as an "agreement," which in turn "is incompatible and inconsistent with the powers conferred on the federal government," he was guilty of inconsistency, unless, that is, the Constitution was guilty of inconsistency in granting the treaty-making power to the Federal Government and in permitting the States to make agreements with foreign governments subject to the consent of the Congress.

Referring to the limitations placed upon state power by the tenth section of the first article of the Constitution, Taney stated that the limitations in the first paragraph are absolute and unconditional, while the powers forbidden in the second may be exercised with the consent of Congress. And "it is in the second paragraph that the restrictions are found which apply to the case now before us."[31] Pointing out that in expounding the federal Constitution "every word must have its due force, and appropriate meaning; for . . . no word was unnecessarily used or needlessly added,"[32] the Chief Justice asserted that this principle of construction applies with peculiar force to the two clauses of the tenth section of the first article because the whole of this short section is directed to the same subject — to the enumeration of the rights surrendered by the States — and this is done with so much clearness and brevity, that it cannot be believed superfluous words were used or words which meant merely the same thing. "When, therefore, the second clause declares, that no state shall enter into 'any agreement or compact' with a foreign power without the assent of Congress, the words 'agreement' and 'compact' cannot be construed as synonomous with one another; and still less can either of them be held to mean the same thing with the word 'treaty' in the preceding clause, into which the states are positively and unconditionally forbidden to enter; and which even the consent of Congress could not authorize."[33]

The Court subsequently stated with respect to compacts and agreements that it did not "perceive any difference in the meaning, except that the word 'compact' is generally used with reference to more formal and serious engagements than is usually implied in the term 'agreement'. . . ."[34] Moreover, with respect to the same subject matter, as for example, in the case of extradition arrangements, an agreement made by the Federal Government with a foreign government is a "treaty,"[35] while one made by a State with a foreign government must be termed an agreement — if it is to be constitutional.[36]

In the instant case, however, Taney, speaking of the treaty-making power, said that whatever is granted to the general government is forbidden to the States, because the same word is used to describe the power denied to the States which is employed in describing the power conferred on the general government, and, therefore, Vermont could not have entered into a treaty with England, or the Canadian government, by which the State agreed to deliver up fugitives charged with offences committed in Canada.[37] Taney acknowledged that it might be said that this was not a treaty, but he avowed that the question did not rest on the prohibition as to treaties. "In the very next clause of the Constitution, the states are forbidden to enter into any 'agreement' or 'compact' with a foreign nation; and as these words could not have been idly or superfluously used by the framers of the Constitution, they cannot be construed to mean the same thing with the word treaty. They evidently mean something more, and were designed to make the prohibition more comprehensive."[38] Quoting the definitions from Vattel already noted,[39] Taney stated that after reading these extracts, the intention of the Framers of the Constitution in using the words, "treaty," "compact," "agreement" should be evident:

"The word 'agreement,' does not necessarily import any direct and express stipulation; nor is it necessary that it should be in writing. If there is a verbal understanding to which both parties have assented, and upon which both are acting, it is an 'agreement.' And the use of all of these terms, 'treaty,' 'agreement,' 'compact,' show that it was the intention of the framers of the Constitution to use the broadest and most comprehensive terms; and that they anxiously desired to cut off all connection or communication between a state and a foreign power: and we shall fail to execute that evident intention, unless we give to the word 'agreement' its most extended signification; and so apply it as to prohibit every agreement, written or verbal, formal or informal, positive or implied, by the mutual understanding of the parties."[40]

Moreover, Taney indicated that it was not necessary, in order to bring the case within this prohibition, that the agreement should be for the mutual delivery of all fugitives from justice, or for a particular class of fugitives. It was sufficient, if there were an agreement to deliver Holmes. This constitutional prohibition applies not only to a continuing agreement embracing classes or cases, or a succession of cases, but to any agreement whatever.[41] Neither does it matter in the instant case that there is no formal agreement, but rather something that "is, in some way or other, mutually understood by the parties. . . . The Constitution looked to the essence and substance of things, and not to mere form."[42] One of the main objects of the Constitution, Taney stated, was to make us, so far as our foreign relations are concerned, one people and one nation and to cut all communications between foreign governments and the several state authorities. The power claimed for the States he deemed utterly incompatible with that evident intention; it would expose us to one of those dangers against which the Framers of the Constitution so anxiously endeavored to guard.[43]

Because of the division in the Court, it is to be recalled, no judgment was given in the case. A majority of the Court, however, concurred in the opinion that Vermont lacked the power to deliver up to a foreign government a fugitive from justice for a crime committed in that government's territory. The Supreme Court of Judicature of the State of Vermont, after examining the opinions of the Court, concluded that a majority had held the power to surrender Holmes nonexistent in the State and issued a writ of habeas corpus for his discharge.[44]

Taney's opinion had a forerunner with respect to state compacts with foreign nations in dicta of Chief Justice Marshall in *Barron* v. *Baltimore*.[45] The Chief Justice there pointed out that the inhibitions contained in the tenth section and applied in direct words to the States "generally restrain state legislation on subjects entrusted to the general government, or in which the people of all the states feel an interest."[46] A State is forbidden to enter into any treaty, alliance, or confederation. "If these compacts are with foreign nations, they interfere with the treaty making power which is conferred entirely on the general government; if with each other, for political purposes, they can scarcely fail to interfere with the general purpose and intent of the constitution."[47]

The opinion in *Holmes* v. *Jennison* would seem sufficiently broad to interdict any intercourse between the States of the Union and a foreign government. The effect of congressional consent upon the prohibition was not considered. *Holmes* v. *Jennison,* it should be noted, was concerned with extradition, and its language must be considered in that connection.[48] Marshall's dictum in *Barron* v. *Baltimore,* too, would appear to indicate that any state compact of a political nature with a foreign nation would be precluded as an interference with the federal treaty-making power. The conclusion that all compacts, political and non-political, are precluded must be balanced against the express constitutional provision: "No State shall, without the consent of Congress, . . . enter into any agreement or compact . . . with a foreign power. . . ." That same provision renders it impossible to conclude that the distinction between treaties and compacts lies in the fact that treaties are made with foreign governments. It may be that the political consideration alluded to in most of the cases treated affords the key to the solution.

It should be recalled that the Court in *Virginia* v. *Tennessee* quoted Story's distinction with approval[49] and indicated that some interstate arrangements would not require the consent of Congress. Furthermore, state courts have based decisions on the distinction and the dicta in *Virginia* v. *Tennessee. McHenry County* v. *Brady*[50] is one such state case. In this case, the highest court of the State of North Dakota sustained action on the part of a local subdivision of the State of North Dakota without congressional consent to obtain the consent of the local government opposite it in Canada to the construction of a drain for the removal of surface waters. The Court admitted that *Holmes* v. *Jennison* used quite sweeping language in regard to the clause in question, but observed that the case was one which involved the right of extradition, essentially a national and governmental power, and that the Court's language must be construed in connection with the subject under consideration. "Although, indeed there is language in that case which seems to preclude any intercourse between a state and a foreign state, the later decisions of the court seem to adopt the theory that not all intercourse is forbidden, or contracts prohibited, but only those agreements or compacts which affect the supremacy of the United

States, or its political rights, or which tend in any measure to increase the political power of the states as against the United States or between themselves."[51] In the *McHenry County* case the court deemed the prohibitions of section 10 to be directed against the formation of any combination tending to the increase of political power in the States, which might affect the supremacy of the United States. Clause 3 of section 10 is not concerned with agreements which in no way affect that supremacy and which are in no way political. The obtainment of the consent of the authorities of the neighboring State or nation to the construction of the drain for the removal of surface waters, which without the drain could be permitted to flow across the national boundary, is an arrangement which does not affect the supremacy of the United States and is in no way political.[52] The case was never brought before the Supreme Court for review and correction, if correction were deemed necessary. Repetition of the dicta of *Virginia* v. *Tennessee* in case after case renders it questionable whether any correction were necessary. This, of course, is based upon the assumption that dicta frequently quoted with approval over a long period of time point the direction in which the Court is moving.

The Court has narrowed the range within which the distinction between a treaty and a compact falls. In each case where a compact has been sustained the Court has indicated to that extent the area of the permissible. In the case of *Wharton v. Wise*[53] the Court considered the validity of the compact of 1785 between Virginia and Maryland, which, among other things, extended to citizens of the latter State the privilege of oyster fishing in certain of the waters of Virginia. The validity of the compact was questioned on two counts: (1) as in conflict with the clause of the Articles of Confederation which provided that no two or more States should enter into any treaty, confederation or alliance whatever between them without the consent of the United States in Congress assembled, specifying accurately the purposes for which the same was to be entered into and how long it should continue; and (2) as having been superseded by the Constitution of the United States subsequently adopted. The Court stated initially with respect to these positions that the clause of the Articles prohibiting any treaty, confederation, or alliance between the States without the consent of Congress was intended to prevent any union of two or more States having a tendency to break up or weaken the league between the whole. It was not designed to prevent arrangements between adjoining States to facilitate the free intercourse of their citizens or remove barriers to their peace and prosperity, and "whatever their effect, such arrangements could not be the subject of complaint by the States making them until, at least, the Congress of the Confederation interposed objections to their adoption or enforcement, which was never done." The provisions of such a compact, so far as they were inconsistent with the Constitution of the United States, subsequently adopted, would be suspended and superseded by it.[54] This compact remained when the Confederation ceased to exist "as an operative agreement, binding the action of the two States upon the subjects embraced, where not inconsistent with the Constitution. . . ."[55] In the nature of dicta the Court quoted with approval the language of *Virginia* v. *Tennessee* and applied it to the Articles of Confederation, stating that it was clear that the prohibition of the Articles of Confederation was not directed against agreements of the character expressed by the compact under consideration. "Its execution could in no respect encroach upon or weaken the general authority of Congress under those articles."[56] It pointed out, too, that under the Confederation various compacts were entered into between Pennsylvania and New Jersey and between Pennsylvania and Virginia in reference to boundaries between them, to rights of fishery in their waters, and to titles to land in their respective States, without the consent of Congress, which indicated that such consent was not deemed essential to their validity. The States of Virginia and Maryland were sovereign with no common superior and no tribunal to determine for them the true construction and meaning of the compact's provisions in case of a conflict of opinion upon the subject. Congress could have interposed objections to adoption or enforcement of the compact of 1785 as being within the meaning of the terms treaty or confederation, or as establishing an alliance within the prohibition of the articles mentioned, but it did not do so. And it would not lie in either of the States that were parties to the contract to allege its invalidity on the subject. The Court concluded that the compact of 1785 was not prohibited by the Articles of Confederation, that it was not a treaty, confederation, or alliance within the meaning of those terms as there used, that it remained as a subsisting operative contract between them in full force when the Confederation went out of existence upon the adoption of the Constitution, and that it was not affected or set aside by the prohibitory clause of that instrument. The prohibition of the Constitution "extends only to future agreements or compacts, not against those already in existence, except so far as their stipulations might affect subjects placed under the control of Congress, such as commerce and the navigation of public waters, which is included under the power to regulate commerce."[57]

Where the Compact Clause Applies. What compacts or agreements are so constituted as to fall within the scope of the constitutional provision requiring congressional consent for their validity? Compacts involving interstate boundaries have come before the Supreme Court many times. The Court's decisions and observations relative to such compacts clarify their status with respect to the Compact Clause and indicate that they fall within its purview.

In the case of *Poole* v. *Fleeger*[58] the Court considered on writ of error an action in ejectment instituted by Fleeger against Poole to recover a tract of land held under a Virginia military land warrant. Poole claimed the lands under North Carolina and Tennessee titles. By a compact sanctioned by Congress, Kentucky and Tennessee in 1820 established their joint boundary, acknowledging that the territory in which the lands involved in the instant case lay belonged to Tennessee. By the terms of the compact the titles to lands held under Virginia military land warrants and under Kentucky grants were confirmed. The circuit court of the United States for the district of West Tennessee instructed the jury that the State of Tennessee, by sanctioning the compact, admitted that the lands in dispute were, at the time they were granted, not within her jurisdiction, nor within that of North Carolina, and that, consequently, the titles were subject to the conditions of the compact. The defendants excepted to this opinion, and the validity of their exception constituted the main subject of inquiry before the Court in the instant case, the jury having rendered a verdict favorable to Fleeger on the basis of this opinion and the court having rendered judgment in conformity thereto. The Supreme Court sustained that judgment, holding that the instructions of the circuit court to the jury were entirely correct. Mr. Justice Story, speaking for the Court, stated that it could not be doubted that it is a part of the general right of sovereignty belonging to independent nations to establish and fix disputed boundaries between their respective territories, and the boundaries so established and fixed by compact between nations become conclusive upon all the subjects and citizens thereof and bind their rights and are to be treated, for all intents and purposes, as the real and true boundaries. Moreover, that right belongs equally to the States of the Union, unless it was surrendered under the Constitution. It was not so surrendered. "So far from there being any pretence of such a general surrender of the right, . . . it is expressly recognized by the constitution, and guarded in its exercise by a single limitation or restriction, requiring the consent of congress. The constitution declares, that 'No state shall, without the consent of congress, enter into any agreement or compact with another state;'

thus, plainly admitting that, with such consent, it might be done. . . ."[59]

The opinion of the Court in *Rhode Island* v. *Massachusetts*[60] clearly indicated that agreements and compacts as to boundaries constitute agreements and compacts within the meaning of those words as used in the Compact Clause. The Court in this case decreed that it possessed jurisdiction and could entertain the case presented by the Massachusetts-Rhode Island boundary dispute.[61] The Court observed that under the tenth section of the first article of the Constitution the States had surrendered the power of settling contested boundaries either by war, or in peace by compact or agreement without the permission of Congress. If Congress consented, then the States were in this respect restored to their original inherent sovereignty, requirement of that consent being the sole limitation imposed by the Constitution. With congressional consent their compact became of binding force and settled the boundary between them, operating with the same effect as a treaty between sovereign powers.[62] "In looking to the practical construction of this clause of the constitution, relating to agreements and compacts by the states," the Court observed with respect to its scope, "in submitting those which relate to boundaries to congress for its consent, its giving its consent, and the action of this Court upon them; it is most manifest, that by universal consent and action, the words 'agreement' and 'compact' are construed to include those which relate to boundary; yet that word boundary is not used. No one has ever imagined that compacts of boundary were excluded, because not expressly named; on the contrary, they are held by the states, congress, and this Court, to be included by necessary implication; the evident consequence resulting from their known object, subject matter, the context, and historical reference to the state of the times and country."[63] The Court asserted that no such exception had been thought of, as it would render the clause a perfect nullity for all practical purposes, especially that "evidently intended" by the Constitution in the grant to Congress of the power of dissenting to such compacts. That intent was "Not to prevent the states from settling their own boundaries, so far as merely affected their relations to each other, but to guard against the derangement of their federal relations with the other states of the Union, and the federal government; which might be injuriously affected, if the contracting states might act upon their boundaries at their pleasure."[64] The Court noted that only two tribunals under the Constitution could act on the boundaries of States, Congress or the judicial power. The former was limited in express terms to assent or dissent, where a compact or agreement was referred to it by the States; and as the latter could be exercised only by the Supreme Court, when a State was a party, the power was either in the Court or non-existent.[65]

In the case of *Virginia* v. *Tennessee* the State of Virginia asked that the compact entered into by her and the State of Tennessee, as set forth in the act of the general assembly of Virginia of January 22, 1803, and which became operative by similar action of the legislature of Tennessee on the 3d of November following,[66] be set aside as null and void on the ground that it was entered into without the consent of Congress.

An interesting though incidental point was the Court's indication of the fine line beyond which an arrangement with respect to boundaries becomes an agreement or compact within the meaning of the Constitution's Compact Clause:

"The mere selection of parties to run and designate the boundary line between two States, or to designate what line should be run, of itself imports no agreement to accept the line run by them, and such action of itself does not come within the prohibition. Nor does a legislative declaration, following such a line, that it is correct, and shall thereafter be deemed the true and established line, import by itself a contract or agreement with the adjoining State. It is a legislative declaration which the State and individuals, affected by the recognized boundary line, may invoke against the State as an admission, but not as a compact or agreement."[67]

Unilateral legislation, then, does not constitute an agreement; the word implies bilateral or multilateral action; the element of reciprocity or "mutual declaration" is necessary. "The legislative declaration will take the form of an agreement or compact when it recites some consideration for it from the other party affected by it, for example, as made upon a similar declaration of the border or contracting State. The mutual declarations may then be reasonably treated as made upon mutual consideration."[68]

Yet, this does not mean that the resultant agreement is such that it requires the consent of Congress for its validity. "The compact or agreement will then be within the prohibition of the Constitution or without it, according as the establishment of the boundary line may lead or not to the increase of the political power or influence of the States affected, and thus encroach or not upon the full and free exercise of Federal authority."[69] If the boundary change is such that it adds to a State an "important and valuable portion" of another, "the political power of the State enlarged would be affected by the settlement of the boundary; and to an agreement for the running of such a boundary, or rather for its adoption afterwards, the consent of

Congress may well be required."[70] On the other hand, if the boundary change has no effect upon the political influence of either State but serves merely to mark and define that which actually existed before, but was undefined and unmarked, the agreement to survey the line and its actual survey would in no respect displace the relation of either of the States to the general government.[71] Applying this reasoning to the instant case, the Court stated that there was, therefore, no compact or agreement between the States which required the consent of Congress for its validity until the States had passed upon the report of the commissioners, ratified their action, and mutually declared the boundary established by them to be the true and real boundary between the States. That ratification was mutually made by each State in consideration of the ratification of the other. Congressional approval then became necessary to render the compact valid, and that approval was fairly to be implied from subsequent legislation and proceedings treating the boundary so established as the true boundary.[72] It may be recalled that the Court sustained the compact in issue, denying Virginia's prayer that it be set aside and annulled and that a new boundary line be run.[73]

An example of a case in which it was held that the agreement in issue was not such that it required the consent of Congress for its validity is afforded by the Louisiana case of *Fisher* v. *Steele*.[74] This case serves to narrow the "penumbra"[75] separating arrangements constituting agreements or compacts within the meaning of the Constitution and those not so. Louisiana authorized the construction of a levee in the State of Arkansas, if Arkansas consented, to protect Louisiana lands from flood waters. The Louisiana Supreme Court sustained the statute authorizing the action against the objection that it was in violation of the Compact Clause of the federal Constitution. The court stated that "On reading that objection in connection with the constitutional prohibition . . . , the mind would naturally expect a charge that the state of Louisiana was projecting a treaty of alliance with the state of Arkansas, or contemplating some joint scheme of commercial or industrial enterprise, or perhaps conspiring for the establishment of a new confederacy; but great is the relief when the mind is informed that the purpose which the plaintiff resists with such a powerful shield is merely to build a piece of levee in the state of Arkansas, if necessary, and if that state does not object, or consents. It is indeed too clear for argument that such a transaction is no more a prohibited compact between two states than is contained in the requisition of one governor for, and the consent of another to, the capture and arrest of a fugitive from justice."[76] The court's reasoning in this case appears to be faulty in two respects. If a State surrenders a fugitive from justice to another State, the State merely complies with the constitutional mandate contained in section 2 of Article IV of the Constitution, which prescribes that "A Person charged in any State with Treason, Felony, or other Crime, who shall flee from Justice, and be found in another State, shall on Demand of the executive Authority of the State from which he fled, be delivered up, to be removed to the State having Jurisdiction of the Crime." The court's analogy is not analogous. Moreover, a State may not enter any "Treaty, Alliance, or Confederation" even with the consent of Congress. Hence the court's "horrendous horrible" is not pertinent to whether a compact or agreement may be made without congressional consent. The court should have pointed its reasoning rather to prove this a minor agreement—one not calculated to promote the "formation of any combination tending to the increase of political power in the States, which may encroach upon or interfere with the just supremacy of the United States"—and, hence, not subject to the requirement of congressional consent imposed by the Compact Clause.

Relation to the Obligation of Contracts Clause. Is an interstate agreement or compact a contract within the meaning of the contract impairment clause of the Constitution?[77] This question came up for consideration in connection with *Green* v. *Biddle*[78] and was answered in the affirmative. In this case the Court considered and held certain acts of Kentucky concerning occupying claimants of land repugnant to the Constitution of the United States, as being in violation of the Virginia-Kentucky compact insofar as they affected the lands covered by that compact. The Court observed that a slight effort to prove that a compact between two States does not present a case within the meaning of the Constitution, which speaks of contracts, had been made but not much pressed. The Court brushed aside that effort, flatly stating that the duty, not less than the power of the Court to declare unconstitutional a law which impairs the obligation of contracts, whoever might be the parties to them, was too clearly enjoined by the Constitution itself and too firmly established by the decisions of the Court and of other courts to be shaken, and that "those decisions entirely cover the present case." The Court defined a contract as the agreement of two or more parties to do or not to do certain acts, and asserted that it was obvious that the propositions offered and agreed to by Virginia, being accepted and ratified by Kentucky, constituted a contract.[79] The Court pointed out that the terms compact and contract are synonomous, substantiating its statement with the observaion that in *Fletcher* v. *Peck* Chief Justice Marshall defined a contract as a compact between two or more parties.[80] The principles enunciated in *Fletcher* v. *Peck*[81] were "that the constitution of the United States embraces all contracts, executed or executory, whether between individuals, or between a state and individuals; and that a state has no more power to impair an obligation into which she herself has entered, than she can the contracts of individuals." Kentucky, therefore, being a party to the compact which guaranteed to claimants of land lying in that State, under titles derived from Virginia, their rights as they existed under the laws of Virginia, was incompetent to violate that contract by passing any law which rendered those rights less valid and secure.[82] The Kentucky acts concerning occupying claimants of land which precipitated the instant case, being challenged, were declared "repugnant to the constitution of the United States."[83]

The seventh article of the Virginia-Kentucky compact declared "that all rights and interests of land, within the said district, derived from the laws of Virginia, shall remain valid and secure, under the laws of the proposed state, and shall be determined by the laws now existing in this state."[84] It was further contended that, if the entire compact were not invalid, at least this article of it was so, as it surrendered inalienable rights of sovereignty. The Court replied that this objection rested upon a principle, the correctness of which remained to be proved, stating that it was practically opposed by the theory of all limited governments, and especially of those constituting the Union. The legislative powers granted to the general government and to the several state governments by their respective constitutions are all limited. In fact, the Court pointed out, the article of the federal Constitution involved in the instant case was one, among many others, of the restrictions alluded to. If it should be answered that those limitations were imposed by the people in their sovereign character, it might be asked if the acceptance of the Virginia-Kentucky compact were not the act of the people of Kentucky in their sovereign character. The compact was contained in an act of the Virginia legislature passed the 18th of December, 1789, and ratified by the convention which framed the constitution of Kentucky and incorporated into that constitution as one of its fundamental articles.

The Virginia-Kentucky compact was before the Court again in *Hawkins* v. *Barney's Lessee*,[85] where the Court sustained, against allegations of invalidity, a Kentucky statute which changed to seven years the time period in which suits for the recovery of lands might be brought. Virginia law at the time of the compact's negotiation prescribed a twenty-year limit for the right. The Court reviewed *Green* v. *Biddle* and pointed out that upon looking through the course of legislation in Virginia and finding no principle or precedent to support such laws, the Court passed upon them as "laws calculated in effect to annihilate the rights secured by the compact, while they avoided an avowed collision with its literal meaning." But in all its reasoning on the subject, the Court will be found to acknowledge, that "whatever course of legislation could be sanctioned by the principles and practice of Virginia, would be regarded as an unaffected compliance with the compact."[86] The Court pointed out that it could scarcely be supposed that Kentucky would have consented to accept a limited and crippled sovereignty, and that it would be unjust to Virginia to believe that she would have wished to reduce Kentucky to a state of vassalage.

But, if the literal and rigid construction necessary to preclude passage of the statute at issue were to be adopted, it would be difficult to assign to Kentucky a position higher than that of a Virginia dependent. If the language of the compact were literally applied, there would be presented the anomaly of a sovereign State governed by the laws of another sovereign, of one half the territory of a sovereign State hopelessly and forever subjected to the laws of another State — a diversity of laws under which A would be subject to one class of laws because holding under a Virginia grant, while B, his next door neighbor, claiming from Kentucky would hardly be conscious of living under the same government. It is to be noted, however, that this case involved merely the construction of the compact, and the Court chose to construe it in such a way as to permit upholding the statute, the validity of which was in question.

Jurisdiction of the Federal Courts. Numerous questions have been considered and answered by the Court relative to the jurisdiction of the federal courts in cases involving compacts.

The Court divided equally in *Holmes* v. *Jennison*[87] upon the issue of whether it possessed jurisdiction in a case involving an extradition arrangement between a State and a foreign government. Chief Justice Taney, in an opinion in which three of his colleagues concurred, pointed out that the Governor of Vermont issued a warrant for the detention of Holmes, a fugitive from justice in Canada, and commanded his surrender to the Canadian authorities. The validity of the Governor's warrant was drawn into question upon the ground that the authority of the Governor to issue the order for the arrest of Holmes and his transportation to a foreign country was repugnant to the United States Constitution. The highest court of the State decided in favor of the validity of the authority so exercised. "Here, then," the Chief Justice stated, "is precisely one of the cases in which the writ of error is given in the twenty-fifth section of the act of 1789."[88] Four others of Taney's colleagues, in four separate opinions, disagreed with his view,[89] however, and the writ of error was dismissed. Taney's opinion — with which a majority agreed on this point — considered exercise of the power to surrender Holmes non-existent in the State, and the Supreme Court of Judicature of the State of Vermont, concluding that this was the holding of the Court, issued a writ of habeas corpus for Holmes' discharge. The important point for our consideration at this stage is that the Court divided equally on the question of whether the case fell within its jurisdiction.

Subsequently, the Court stated that "it can hardly be admitted that . . . the extradition of a fugitive from justice can become the subject of negotiation between a state of this Union and a foreign government."[90] The Court pointed out that treaties existed with almost all the countries with which they would be likely to be necessary and that the treaties were supplemented by acts of Congress, both of which "are in their nature exclusive."[91] Hence the question of jurisdiction over cases involving extradition arrangements between a State and a foreign government has been made of no significance by prohibition of the arrangements themselves.

Another question for consideration is whether a compact becomes a federal law by virtue of congressional consent so as to fall within the meaning of Article III, section 2, clause 1 of the Constitution, which states that "The judicial Power shall extend to all Cases . . . arising under . . . the Laws of the United States," and within the meaning of subsequent legislation enacted to effect that clause. This question, too, has been before the Court. In the case *Pennsylvania* v. *Wheeling & Belmont Bridge Co.*[92] the Court considered a bill brought by a State to restrain a public nuisance in the form of the erection of a bridge across the Ohio River, which was alleged to be of insufficient elevation to permit unobstructed navigation of the river. Pennsylvania's interest was deemed sufficiently direct to sustain an application to the Supreme Court in the exercise of original jurisdiction for an injunction to remove the obstruction. The bridge was constructed under authority of a Virginia statute, which, it was admitted, conferred full authority subject to the plenary power of Congress to regulate interstate commerce. But Congress had acted here. It had sanctioned the Virginia-Kentucky compact guaranteeing free use and navigation of the Ohio. Virginia's statute was in conflict with the acts of Congress which were the paramount law. The compact, by the sanction of Congress, had become "a law of the Union." A state law violating it was unconstitutional.[93] The Court pointed out that in *Green* v. *Biddle* the Court had held void a law of the State of Kentucky in violation of the compact between Virginia and Kentucky and had declared that the Court possessed authority to declare a state law unconstitutional upon the ground of its impairing the obligation of a compact between States of the Union.

Congress subsequently passed an act authorizing the bridge, however, and the case came before the Court once more. In the decision the Court again said that the basis of the earlier decision was that the act of Virginia afforded no authority or justification. It was in "conflict with the acts of congress, which were the paramount law."[94] According to this language an interstate compact "by the sanction of Congress" becomes a "law of the Union." The Court indicated that the intervening act of Congress declaring the bridges over the Ohio River to be lawful structures and requiring vessels to navigate so as not to interfere with them was within the legitimate exercise by Congress of its constitutional power to regulate commerce. That act was sustained against allegations of invalidity on the ground of conflict with the Virginia-Kentucky compact in respect to the free navigation of the Ohio River and on the ground of conflict with the constitutional provision that "no preference shall be given by any regulation of commerce or revenue to the ports of one State over those of another."[95]

In the first *Wheeling Bridge* case Congress was sanctioning a compact which affected interstate commerce, however, and hence its sanction was expressive of its will with respect to that commerce. If the compact had related to drainage, it might well be asked whether the effect of congressional sanction would have been considered the same in making the compact a "law of the Union." Perhaps the answer is afforded by the Court's opinion in the case below.

In *People* v. *Central Railroad*[96] the Court was called upon to consider a case arising out of the agreement of 1833 between New York and New Jersey relative to their joint boundary. Congress assented to the agreement by an act approved June 28th, 1834. Subsequently, the "People" of the State of New York sued a New Jersey corporation for taking possession of territory which New York claimed was within its jurisdiction. The corporation claimed, however, that, under the terms of the agreement, the territory in question was within the jurisdiction of New Jersey, and the highest tribunal of New York decided in favor of the corporation's claim. From that decision a writ of error was taken on the ground that the judgment was against the rights of New York as defined by the agreement, and that the Supreme Court had jurisdiction "because of the act giving the assent of Congress to it."[97] The Court in a short but clear and unequivocal opinion dismissed the case, denying jurisdiction, because the statement of the case showed that the question arose under the agreement and not under an act of Congress. "The assent of Congress did not make the act giving it a statute of the United States, in the sense of the 25th section of the Judiciary Act."[98] The Court stated that the construction of the act granting congressional consent to the compact was in no way drawn in question, nor had any title or right been set up under it and denied by the state court. The act had no effect beyond giving the consent of Congress to the compact between the two States. The writ of error accordingly was dismissed. This holding, then, indicates that a compact itself is not by virtue of its congressional sanction a federal statute, such as would support the jurisdiction of the federal courts in cases relative to construction of its meaning.[99]

In the case of *Kentucky Union Co.* v. *Kentucky,*[100] however, the Court sustained the Revenue and Taxation Act of Kentucky of March 5, 1906, against allegations of invalidity on the grounds that it was an *ex post facto* law, deprived landowners of their property without due process of law, denied them equal protection of the law, and violated the provisions of the Virginia-Kentucky compact of 1789. Three cases were treated together by the Court. Two of the cases grew out of action brought by the State for forfeiture of lands because of the failure of the owners to list and pay taxes upon them in compliance with the requirements of the law drawn in issue in the instant case. The other grew out of a petition for assessment and taxation of lands in controversy, brought by a company claiming to own them under Virginia patents. Although the petition was dismissed for failure to conform to the requirements of law, the Kentucky court found the constitutionality of the act in question necessarily involved and decided in its favor. The cases then came before the Supreme Court of the United States on writs of error. The Court stated with respect to the contract impairment allegation that "Another ground of objection under the Federal Constitution is insisted upon in the alleged violation of the Virginia Compact of 1789, embodied in the constitution of Kentucky, and held by this court to be a binding contract between the States."[101] The Court reviewed the cases of *Green* v. *Biddle* and *Hawkins* v. *Barney's Lessee*[102] and pointed out that the effect of those decisions was to declare that while the Virginia compact prevented the cutting down of the titles secured under the State of Virginia prior to its date, so as to take away substantial rights incident to those titles, as was the case in *Green* v. *Biddle,* it did not mean to prevent the

State, upon notice and hearing, from requiring the registration of land titles for taxation, or in default thereof, from forfeiting such titles to the State. Such laws did not have the effect of taking away legitimate rights secured by the old grants but merely enabled the new sovereign to enforce the taxing laws of the State against such lands, as well as others. The Court observed that it was recognized that the land would pass under the dominion of the new State which would require revenues for its support, and, while the title obtained from the State of Virginia was protected, it was not intended that that title should be immune from constitutional laws subjecting such lands to the taxing power of the new sovereignty and requiring their owners by all proper methods to contribute their share to the public burdens of the State. The act's provisions which were in issue were sustained. The Court had exercised its jurisdiction and had considered the "meaning" of the compact involved. This exercise was not in conflict with the holding of the Court in *People* v. *Central Railroad,* but it emphasized that the application of that decision in restricting the Court's exercise of jurisdiction was limited. The allegation of contract impairment brings the issue within the realm of federal questions, and subjects the meaning of the compact involved to judicial scrutiny by the Court.

This is borne out by the decision of the Court in *Kentucky* v. *Indiana,*[108] a case falling within the original jurisdiction of the Supreme Court because a controversy between States. Kentucky brought suit in the Supreme Court against Indiana on a contract for the construction of a bridge across the Ohio River, to which the consent of Congress had been obtained. Suit had been brought in an Indiana court by Indiana taxpayers and citizens to restrain the State's compliance with the contract on the ground that it was void because without authorization in Indiana law. The Kentucky bill prayed that Indiana be required to perform the obligation of its contract and the Indiana citizens be enjoined from prosecution of their suit. Indiana admitted the validity of the contract and pointed to the local litigation and her desire legally to establish her authority to perform the contract as the reason for non-performance of her obligation. Moreover, she indicated that, if Kentucky were granted the relief requested, she would immediately perform her contractual obligation. The private citizens of Indiana who were involved, however, contested both the jurisdiction of the Supreme Court and the validity of the compact. The Court dismissed the bill as to the individual citizens of Indiana, indicating that a State's citizens, voters, and taxpayers, as such, without a showing of further and proper interest, possess no separate individual right to contest in such a suit the position taken by the State itself. The

Court then entertained the suit as "a controversy between the States, although a limited one." [104] Moreover, the Court pointed out that it could not be gainsaid that in a controversy with respect to a contract between States, as to which the original jurisdiction of the Court was invoked, the Court possessed the authority and duty to determine for itself all questions pertaining to the obligations of the contract alleged. The fact that the solution of those questions might involve determination of the effect of local legislation of either State, as well as of acts of Congress, said to authorize the contract, in no way affects the duty of the Court to act as the final, constitutional arbiter in deciding the questions properly presented. The Court concluded that the controversy between the States was within the original jurisdiction of the Court, that the defendant State had shown no adequate defense to the suit, that nothing had appeared which would justify delay in rendering a decree, and that the Commonwealth of Kentucky was entitled to the relief sought against the State of Indiana.

It might well be desirable to bring the adjudication of all rights under compacts within the province of the federal courts. In that way the "anomaly" alluded to by counsel in the brief for Kentucky in *Kentucky* v. *Indiana* could be precluded. Kentucky counsel pointed out that it would be an anomaly if a contract entered into by the proper officers pursuant to legislative authority could be declared invalid by the courts of either State; for, if that were the rule, the courts of one State might hold the contract to be valid, and the courts of the other State might hold it to be invalid. [105] In the instant case that result was impossible because the fact that the case presented a controversy between States rendered it subject to decision by the Supreme Court. This would settle counsel's fears as to a case to which States are parties. The observation of Kentucky counsel could be directed to cases in which the States themselves were not parties. But even there the feared result might be avoided by bringing the issue within the jurisdiction of the federal judiciary by an allegation of contract impairment, or, if the contestants were from two States, under diversity of citizenship.

Controversies over agreements concerning interstate boundaries have been recognized as presenting federal questions. In *Cissna* v. *Tennessee* [106] the Court stated in reference to a Tennessee judgment that the Tennessee court was in error in deciding that a question of boundary had been settled by the duly constituted authorities of the two States by judicial decisions, legislation, long acquiescence, exercise of jurisdiction, and other acts amounting to an agreement or convention defining the limit between the States to be the line midway between the visible banks of the river. "Obviously, whether two States of the Union, either by long acquiescence in a practical location of their common boundary, or by agreement otherwise evidenced, have definitely fixed or changed the limits of their jurisdiction as laid down by the authority of the general Government in treaty or statute,[107] is in its nature a federal question."[108]

While the foregoing case refers specifically to state boundaries as determined by trealy or statute, an unqualified statement of the principle that controversies over agreements concerning interstate boundaries present federal questions is afforded by the opinion of the Court in the case of *Virginia* v. *West Virginia,*[109] where a question raised by West Virginia as to the judicial nature of boundary disputes was disposed of by the Court with the observation that "This proposition cannot be sustained without reversing the settled course of decision in this court and overturning the principles on which several well-considered cases have been decided."[110] The Court then noted that the "established doctrine of this court" is "that it has jurisdiction of questions of boundary between two States of this Union, and that this jurisdiction is not defeated, because in deciding that question it becomes necessary to examine into and construe compacts or agreements between those States, or because the decree which the court may render, affects the territorial limits of the political jurisdiction and sovereignty of the States which are parties to the proceeding."[111]

In accord with this decision is that in the case of *Wedding* v. *Meyler*[112] where the Court considered the question of the extent of Indiana's jurisdiction over the Ohio River. Indiana's jurisdiction was derived from the Virginia-Kentucky compact and the federal statute admitting Kentucky into the Union which gave consent to that compact. In deciding that Indiana had concurrent jurisdiction with Kentucky on the section of the Ohio bordering upon it, the Court construed the Virginia compact. An Indiana judgment dependent for its vadidity upon a summons served on that part of the river is entitled to full faith and credit when sued upon in another State. The effect of the compact and the federal statute involved in granting jurisdiction to Indiana was deemed a federal question. This would have been so if for no other reason than that determination of this question was necessary to the exercise of "full faith and credit" jurisdiction.

Controversies concerning rights in interstate streams have also been held to fall within the jurisdiction of the federal judiciary as "presenting federal questions." In *Hinderlider* v. *La Plata Co.*[113] the Court reaffirmed the holding of *People* v. *Central Railroad* with respect to the nature of a compact, stating that "The assent of Congress to the compact between Colorado and New Mexico does not make it a 'treaty or statute of the United States' within the meaning of § 237 (a) of the Judicial Code. . . ."[114] Moreover, the Court stated that no question as to the validity of the consent was presented. The Court deemed this no basis for entertainment of the appeal. The Court pointed out, however, that in holding that the water officials of the State should be enjoined from taking action required by the compact, the state court denied an important claim under the Constitution which might be reviewed on certiorari by the Court under § 237 (b).[115] The decision in the state court necessarily rested on the premise that Colorado was entitled to a set amount of water, regardless of the amount left for New Mexico, and could not stand if that determination were erroneous. The Court then stated that "whether the water of an interstate stream must be apportioned between the two States is a question of 'federal common law' upon which neither the statutes nor the decisions of either State can be conclusive. . . . Jurisdiction over controversies concerning rights in interstate streams is not different from those concerning boundaries."[116] Controversies "concerning boundaries," the Court continued, "have been recognized as presenting federal question."[117] *Cissna* v. *Tennessee* was cited.[118] Moreover, the Court stated, "The decisions are not uniform as to whether the interpretation of an interstate compact presents a federal question."[119]

The Court resolved the issue of jurisdiction over cases involving interstate compacts in *Delware River Joint Toll Bridge Commission* v. *Colburn,*[120] where it held that the construction of an interstate compact sanctioned by congressional statute involves a federal "title, right, privilege or immunity" which, when "specially set up and claimed" in a state court, may be reviewed by the Supreme Court. In this case the Court deemed "the questions of the construction of the Compact between states" and of its jurisdiction of "public importance" sufficient to warrant the grant of certiorari.[121] The Court referred to *People* v. *Central Railroad,* stating that in that case "jurisdiction of this Court to review a judgment of a state court construing a compact between states was denied on the ground that the Compact was not a statute of the United States and that the construction of the Act of Congress giving consent was in no way drawn in question, nor was any right set up under it." The Court observed that "This decision has long been doubted."[122] It pointed to the footnote in the case of *Hinderlider* v. *La Plata,* wherein it was stated, upon the basis of the contrast afforded by the decision in *People* v. *Central Railroad* and those in *Wedding* v. *Meyler* and *Wharton* v. *Wise,* that "The decisions are not uniform as to whether the interpretation of an interstate compact presents a federal question."[123] After this judicial criticism of the decision in *People* v. *Central Railroad,* the Court stated that "we now conclude that the construction of such a compact sanctioned by Congress by virtue of Article I, § 10, Clause 3 of the Constitution, involves a federal 'title, right, privilege or immunity' which when 'specially set up and claimed' in a state court may be reviewed here on certiorari under § 237 (b) of the Judicial Code, 28 U. S. C. § 344."[124] The Court then proceeded to consider the language of the compact involved to determine the merits of the arguments presented by the litigants in the instant case. This is the only purpose for which it might conceivably be advantageous to have such a compact considered a "law of the Union," as state legislation enacted by parties to the compact contrary to the compact's terms is invalid without the compact's being a federal "law."

In the 1951 case of *West Virginia ex rel Dyer* v. *Sims*[125] the Court reaffirmed its possession of the power to pass upon the meaning and validity of compacts between States.[126] A compact, the Court pointed out, "is after all a legal document," and disputes with respect to its scope and meaning are bound to arise. Such disputes, like disputes between States where there is no compact, fall within the purview of the Court. "It requires no elaborate argument," the Court noted, "to reject the suggestion that an agreement solemnly entered into between States by those who alone have political authority to speak for a State can be unilaterally nullified, or given final meaning by an organ of one of the contracting States. A State cannot be its own ultimate judge in a controversy with a sister State."[127] It is the function and duty of the Supreme Court of the Nation to "determine the nature and scope of obligations as between States, whether they arise through the legislative means of compact or the 'federal common law' governing interstate controversies."[128] Albeit deference is to be shown to what the state supreme court deems the law and policy of its State, deference is one thing, and submission to a State's determination of whether it has undertaken an obligation, what the obligation is, and whether the State may not undertake it under its constitution, quite another. Two prior decisions, said the Court, "make clear . . . that we are free to examine determinations of law by State courts in the limited field where a compact brings in issue the rights of other States and the United States." *Kentucky* v. *Indiana,* where Chief Justice Hughes "could hardly avoid analogizing the situation to that where a question is raised whether a State has impaired the obligation of a contract,"[129] and *Hinderlider* v. *La Plata River* & *Cherry Creek Ditch Co.*[130] were cited. The *Hinderlider* case "makes clear, if authority be needed, that the fact the compact questions reach us on a writ of certiorari rather than by way of an original action brought by a State does not affect the power of this Court."[131] Moreover, said the Court, that the case presents "issues which give this Court jurisdiction to review the State court proceeding, 28 U.S.C. § 1257, needs no discussion after *Delaware River Comm'n.* v. *Colburn,* 310 U.S. 419, 427."[132] That the Court possesses the power to pass upon the meaning and validity of compacts between States and is not bound in the process by the views of the state courts would seem established.

Summary. In summary, it can be said that interstate agreements and compacts and those between States and foreign powers are permissible under the express provision of the Constitution, subject only to the requirement of congressional assent, while treaties, alliances, and confederations are expressly and absolutely prohibited. The two classes of arrangements are not defined in the Constitution. Story wrote that the absolute prohibition as to treaties, alliances, or confederations might be deemed applicable to treaties of a political character, while the Compact Clause might be deemed applicable to arrangements involving "mere private rights of sovereignty."[133] Story's distinction, moreover, was quoted with approval by the Court in *Virginia* v. *Tennessee.* The Supreme Court to some extent has indicated the nature of the distinction by holding certain arrangements to be within the prohibited class and others, subject to congressional consent, to be within the permitted class. Thus, the Southern "Confederacy" has been held to be non-existent in law as a "confederation" within the meaning of the absolute constitutional prohibition. In a dictum in *Virginia* v. *Tennessee* the Court stated also that the constitutional prohibition as to compacts or agreements among the States without the consent of Congress was "directed to the formation of any combination tending to the increase of political power in the States, which may encroach upon or interfere with the just supremacy of the United States."[134]

In the earlier case of *Holmes* v. *Jennison,* Chief Justice Taney stated for the Court that the words "agreements" and "compacts" as used in the Compact Clause could not be construed as being synonymous terms and that neither of them could be held to mean the same thing as the word "treaty," into which the States are unconditionally forbidden to enter and for which even the consent of Congress could not give authority. But Taney so construed the term "agreement" as to "prohibit every agreement, written or verbal, formal or informal, positive or implied, by the mutual understanding of the parties."[135] The interpretation indicated in the above dictum from *Virginia* v.

Tennessee has been reasserted in case after case, however, and thus is well worth notice, if one assumes that dicta frequently quoted with approval over a long period of time point the direction in which the Court is moving.

It is quite plain, then, that the distinction between treaties and compacts cannot be indicated through classification of the former as arrangements with foreign powers, for the Compact Clause envisions compacts or agreements between States and foreign powers. The only distinguishing feature of treaties, alliances, and confederations seems to be their "political" character. This distinction becomes even more tenuous when it is noted that what is a treaty when negotiated by the Federal Government with a foreign power must be a compact, unless void, when negotiated by a State with a foreign power. It must suffice, until the point is clarified further by the Court, that treaties, alliances, and confederations are forbidden to the States and could not be sustained, even if sanctioned by Congress while agreements and compacts made with congressional consent are permitted to them, and that the arrangement establishing the "Confederate States" fell within the former category. The Court has indicated that the Virginia-Maryland compact of 1785, among other things extending fishing privileges in waters under Virginia's jurisdiction to citizens of Maryland, did not fall afoul of the provisions of the Articles of Confederation inhibiting any treaty, confederation, or alliance between the States. The compact "was not a treaty, confederation, or alliance within the meaning of those terms as there used,"[136] because the prohibitory articles were intended to prevent any union between two or more States "having a tendency to break up or weaken the league between the whole" and were not designed to prevent "arrangements" between adjoining States to facilitate the free intercourse of their citizens or to remove barriers to their peace and prosperity. Moreover, the Court stated that the agreement subsisted as an operative contract between the two States insofar as its provisions were consistent with the Constitution, unaffected by the prohibitory clause of that instrument. The constitutional prohibition extends only to future agreements or compacts. Thus, the Court not only differentiated the compact involved from a prohibited treaty, but also indicated the legal status of agreements which antedated the Constitution.

In each case where the Court has sustained an interstate compact, it has blocked out a portion of that nebulous region containing the distinction between the prohibited and the permissible, for treaties, alliances, and confederations could not be sustained, even if sanctioned by Congress.

Although the Constitution couches the Compact Clause in a negative fashion, that is, prohibiting agreements between the States without the consent of Congress, it has been interpreted as implying permission with that consent. Thus, the Court in *Poole* v. *Fleeger* states that "The constitution declares, that 'No state shall, without the consent of congress, enter into any agreement or compact with another state;' thus plainly admitting that, with such consent, it might be done. . . ." [137]

Not only may States enter agreements between themselves with the consent of Congress, but a State, as the Court states in *Stearns* v. *Minnesota*, "may make a compact with all the States, constituting as one body the nation, possessed of general rights of sovereignty and represented by Congress." [138] Thus, the United States may become a party to a compact with one or more of its member States. It would seem odd to consider the resultant arrangement an interstate agreement. But the Court's opinion in this case poses questions which are of interest. [139] Also, in connection with the case of *Stearns* v. *Minnesota*, the Court distinguished between compacts "in reference to political rights and obligations" and "those solely in reference to property belonging to one or the other" of the States and pointed to the fact that different considerations might enter into the question of the validity of the two types.

The contractual character of an interstate compact has precipitated the question of whether it falls within the meaning of the contract impairment clause of the Constitution. Chief Justice Marshall in *Fletcher* v. *Peck* defined a contract as a compact between two or more parties, using the words "compact" and "contract" synonomously, and indicated, moreover, that a State could not impair an obligation into which she had entered any more than she could the contracts of individuals. In *Green* v. *Biddle* the Court stated flatly that the proposition "offered, and agreed to by Virginia, being accepted and ratified by Kentucky, is a contract." [140] Kentucky, then, was prohibited from passing any law which impaired the obligation of that contract, and the laws in question in the instant case were invalidated as "repugnant to the constitution of the United States." [141] Also, in this case the Court rejected the contention that the compact was invalid on the ground that it surrendered rights of sovereignty which are inalienable. The Court pointed out that the contention is "practically opposed by the theory of all limited governments." [142] In *Hawkins* v. *Barney's Lessee*, [143] however, the Court chose to construe the Virginia-Kentucky compact in such a way as to permit upholding a statute allegedly in violation of it, pointing out that it could scarcely be supposed that Kentucky would have consented to accept a limited and crippled sovereignty and that it would be unjust to Virginia to believe that she would have wished to reduce Kentucky to a state of vassalage. The Court pointed to its acknowledgment in *Green* v. *Biddle* that whatever course of legislation could be sanctioned by Virginia principles and practice would be regarded as an "unaffected compliance with the compact." The statute at issue could be so sanctioned and hence was sustained. The treatment of a compact as a contract within the meaning of the contract impairment clause of the Constitution has its advantages and disadvantages, the former as to enforcement, and the latter as to rigidity, possibly rendering the compact device of limited worth for certain contemplated applications. These elements will be considered later in this study.

The Court has considered and answered numerous questions relative to the jurisdiction of the federal judiciary in cases involving interstate compacts. In *Holmes* v. *Jennison* the Court divided equally on the question of whether it could entertain the case. Taney and three of his colleagues thought the facts presented "precisely one of the cases in which the writ of error is given in the twenty-fifth section of the [Judiciary] act of 1789." [144] Four other members of the Court, in four separate opinions, disagreed with that view, and the writ of error was dismissed. A majority of the Court's members could not be mustered to support the view that the case was one in which a writ of error might lie under the "twenty-fifth" section of the Judiciary Act of 1789. It seems clear that cases involving compacts, if they present facts which bring them within the meaning of the "twenty-fifth" section, are within the jurisdiction of the Court. Such facts are presented if the case involves, for example, the contracts clause or the full faith and credit clause. Whether the mere fact of a compact being sanctioned by Congress presents such facts will now be considered.

In early decisions relative to interstate compacts the Court spoke of a compact concerned with navigation of an interstate river as a law of the Union by virtue of its congressional sanction. Thus, the Court stated in the first *Wheeling Bridge* case that "This compact, by the sanction of Congress, has become a law of the Union." [145] Congressional sanction to a compact between Virginia and Kentucky, which provided that the use and navigation of the Ohio, so far as the territory of either State lay thereon, was deemed sufficient to preclude Virginia's authorization of the construction of a bridge interfering with the enjoyment of that use. This sanction constituted congressional regulation of the navigation of the Ohio River, and the fact that it was interstate commerce assured the jurisdiction of the federal courts. It is the general issue of whether a compact becomes a "law of the Union" by congressional sanction so as to support the jurisdiction of the federal judiciary in cases in which it is involved which is signficant.

It might well be questioned whether congressional sanction of a compact relative to drainage, not subject to congressional regulation under its plenary power over interstate commerce, would have been referred to by the Court as a "law of the Union." Treatment of an interstate compact as such as a "law of the Union" has implications, however, which might well be considered. These agreements frequently are not made with respect to subject matter in connection with which the Federal Government has been given power, that is, within the delegated powers of Congress, except the negative power to refuse to sanction the compact. And where they are made with respect to subject matter falling within, or impinging upon, the delegated powers, as, for example, interstate commerce, they are subject to the exercise of those powers by the Federal Government. Moreover, if an administrative agency is established to effectuate the terms of the compact, it is subject to control by the States, rather than the general government. These and other considerations point up the questionable desirability of a determination holding compacts to be laws of the Union. [146]

On the other hand, the anomalous character of permitting state courts to enter final decrees as to the validity of such compacts was indicated by Kentucky counsel in *Kentucky* v. *Indiana,* where it was stated that, "If such were the rule, the courts of one State might hold the contract to be valid and the courts of the other State might hold it to be invalid." [147] In that case the contingency was of no concern, for the case presented "a controversy between the States, although a limited one," and fell within the original jurisdiction of the Court. At any rate, the Court apparently reconsidered the implications of its earlier language and restricted its application to compacts where congressional sanction might be deemed expressive of the will of Congress in the exercise of one of its delegated powers. The *Wheeling Bridge* cases did not indicate that every compact was a "law of the Union" for jurisdictional purposes.

In *People* v. *Central Railroad* the Court denied jurisdiction, stating that "The assent of Congress did not make the act giving it a statute of the United States, in the sense of the 25th section of the Judiciary Act." [148] The Court pointed out that the act giving congressional consent to the compact was in no way drawn in question, and no title or right had been set up under it and denied by the state court. Writ of error does not lie in a case involving a compact simply in virtue of the act giving congressional sanction to that compact. In subsequent cases, however, the Court did entertain cases involving compacts and did consider the meaning of those compacts. In those cases jurisdiction rested upon other grounds than that contended to be its basis in *People* v. *Central Railroad.* The cases serve to emphasize the narrow application of the latter decision in restricting the Court's exercise of jurisdiction. The Court considered the Virginia-Kentucky Compact of 1789 again in the case of *Kentucky Union Co.* v. *Kentucky,* indicating in the process that the allegation of contract impairment brings the issue within the realm of federal questions and subjects the compact involved to judicial scrutiny as to meaning.

In one of the cases under consideration in *Kentucky Union Co.* v. *Kentucky* the Court of Appeals of the State of Kentucky had decided in favor of the state statute, the consitutionality of which had been drawn into question. The Kentucky court's upholding the state statute where its validity was drawn into question on the ground of its being repugnant to the Federal Constitution made the case susceptible to reexamination in the Supreme Court of the United States upon writ of error. Also, in *Kentucky* v. *Indiana* the Court stated that "It can not be gainsaid that in a controversy with respect to a contract between States, as to which the original jurisdiction of this Court is invoked, this Court has the authority and duty to determine for itself all questions that pertain to the obligations of the contract alleged."[149] The Court has recognized that controversies over agreements concerning interstate boundaries present federal questions. In *Cissna* v. *Tennessee* the Court indicated that "whether two States of the Union, either by long acquiescence in a practical location of their common boundary, or by agreement otherwise evidenced, have definitely fixed or changed the limits of their jurisdiction as laid down by the authority of the general Government in treaty or statute, is in its nature a federal question."[150]

In other cases the Court has stated the principle without qualification. In the *Hinderlider* case the Court stated that the decisions as to whether the interpretation of an interstate compact presents a federal question were not uniform. In this case the Court reaffirmed the earlier holding with respect to the nature of a compact, however, indicating that the congressional assent to the Colorado-New Mexico Compact did "not make it a 'treaty or statute of the United States' within the meaning of § 237 (a) of the Judicial Code. . . ."[151] But the question of apportionment of the waters of an interstate stream was one of "federal common law." Pointing to the inconsistency of the decisions on whether the interpretation of an interstate compact presents a federal question, the Court in *Delaware River Joint Toll Bridge Commission* v. *Colburn* stated that the decision in *People* v. *Central Railroad* "has long been doubted." It then proceeded to state that construction of such a compact sanctioned by Congress in conformity with the constitutional requirement "involves a federal 'title, right, privilege or immunity' which when 'specially set up and claimed' in a state court may be reviewed here on certiorari under § 237 (b) of the Judicial Code, 28 U.S.C. § 344."[152] Thus, even if a compact between the States is not by virtue of its congressional consent a "law of the Union," such as to underwrite the Court's review of a state case involving it on writ of error, it involves a federal "title, right, privilege or immunity" which, when "specially set up and claimed" under the United States Constitution in a state court, may be reviewed by the Supreme Court.

In the 1951 case of *West Virginia ex rel Dyer* v. *Sims* the Court reaffirmed its possession of the authority "to pass upon the meaning and validity of compacts" between States. The Court is "free to examine determinations of law by State courts in the limited field where a compact brings in issue the rights of other States and the United States." Nor is the power of the Court affected by the fact that the compact reaches it "on a writ of certiorari rather than by way of an original action brought by a State."[153]

As a result of the chain of cases dealing with jurisdictional questions in respect to compacts, it would seem that almost any case involving a compact could be removed from a state court, which as an instrumentality of the State might conceivably be interested in the outcome of the case, to the federal judiciary.

[1] The provision finally adopted as to the States' arrangements with one another runs: "No two or more states shall enter into any treaty, confederation or alliance whatever between them, without the consent of the united states in congress assembled, specifying accurately the purposes for which the same is to be entered into, and how long it shall continue." *Articles of Confederation*, Article VI, clause 2. "Agreement" is not listed in this clause, while it is listed in that relating to arrangements between States and foreign governments.

[2] A. C. Weinfeld, "What Did the Framers of the Federal Constitution Mean by 'Agreements or Compacts'." *University of Chicago Law Review*, 3:456-57, April, 1936.

[3] *Ibid.*, p. 457. [4] See *ibid.*, pp. 458-60. [5] *Ibid.*, p. 458.

[6] Hugo Grotius, *The Rights of War and Peace*, trans. A. C. Campbell (Washington: M. Walter Dunne, Publisher, 1901), p. 166.

[7] *Ibid.*, p. 167. [8] *Ibid.*

[9] Emmerich de Vattel, *Le Droit des Gens ou Principes de la Loi Naturelle* (Washington: Published by the Carnegie Institution, 1916), I, 369, 397. The translation is Weinfeld's.

[10] Weinfeld, *op. cit.*, p. 460. [11] *Ibid.*, p. 464.

[12] *McCulloch* v. *Maryland*, 4 Wheat. (17 U.S.) 316, 407 (1819).

[13] See *infra*, Ch. V.

[14] Story, *op. cit.*, II, 310. *Cf.* Grotius' view distinguishing "public conventions," which he divides into "treaties, engagements, and other compacts," from the private contracts of individuals and the personal contracts of the sovereigns. See *supra*, Ch. II, pp. 23-24.

[15] *Ibid.*, p. 310. [16] 148 U.S. 503, 528 (1893).

[17] *Ibid.*, p. 520.

[18] See *infra*, Ch. III, for treatment of the case in connection with congressional consent.

[19] *Virginia* v. *Tennessee*, 148 U.S. 503, 517-18 (1893). [20] *Ibid.*, p. 518.

[21] *Ibid.*, p. 519. The dicta of the Court in this case have been born out in many state cour decisions. See *infra*, Ch. III.

[22] See *supra*, Ch. II, p. 25. [23] 6 Otto (96 U.S.) 176 (1877).

[24] *Ibid.*, p. 192. [25] *Ibid.*, p. 182.

[26] *Ibid.* See also *Lamar* v. *Micou*, 112 U.S. 452, 476 (1884), where the Court states: "The so-called Confederate government was in no sense a lawful government, but was a mere government of force, having its origin and foundation in rebellion against the United States. The notes and bonds issued in its name and for its support had no legal value as money or property, except by agreement or acceptance of parties capable of contracting with each other, and can never be regarded by a court sitting under the authority of the United States as securities in which trust funds might be invested."

[27] 14 Pet. (39 U.S.) 540, 614 (1840). [28] *Ibid.*, p. 569.

[29] *Ibid.*, p. 570. [30] *Ibid.*

[31] *Ibid.* [32] *Ibid.*, pp. 570-71.

[33] *Ibid.*, p. 571.

[34] *Virginia* v. *Tennessee*, 148 U.S. 503, 520 (1893).

[35] *United States* v. *Rauscher*, 119 U.S. 407 (1886).

[36] Occasionally the Justices themselves use the terms interchangeably, thereby indicating that the distinction is a rather tenuous one. Thus, Mr. Justice Brandeis, speaking of the Court's suggesting to the parties in interstate boundary disputes that they resort to the compact method, said that: "In *New York* v. *New Jersey*, 256 U.S. 296, 313, which involved a more intricate problem of rights in interstate waters, the recommendation that treaty-making be resorted to was more specific. . . ." *Hinderlider* v. *La Plata Co.*, 304 U.S. 92, 105 (1938).

[37] *Holmes* v. *Jennison*, 14 Pet. (39 U.S.) 540, 614, 571 (1840).

[38] *Ibid.*, pp. 571-72. [39] See *supra*, Ch. II, pp. 24.

[40] *Holmes* v. *Jennison*, 14 Pet. (39 U.S.) 540, 614, 572 (1840).

[41] *Ibid.*, pp. 572-73. Taney's opinion, applying the term "agreement" to "prohibit every agreement, written or verbal, formal or informal, positive or implied, by the mutual understanding of the parties," if considered a general statement, is in marked contrast to that rendered for the Court by Mr. Justice Field in *Virginia* v. *Tennessee*, 148 U.S. 503, 519 (1893), where it was said that "Looking at the clause in which the terms 'compact' or 'agreement' appear, it is evident that the prohibition is directed to the formation of any combination tending to the increase of political power in the States, which may encroach upon or interfere with the just supremacy of the United States." In a dictum in the latter

opinion it was stated that "there are many matters upon which the different States may agree that can in no respect concern the United States." If, however, Taney were thinking and speaking only of political agreements in the foreign relations field, his statement could easily be consistent with the *Virginia* v. *Tennessee* opinion. Only seventeen years later New York made an agreement with Canada to which Congress gave its consent for the chartering of an international bridge corporation, a fact which makes it seem evident that purely non-political agreements between a State and a foreign government were not thought proscribed. See *supra*, Ch. II, pp. 25-27, and for another consideration, *supra*, Ch. II, pp. 29-30.

[42] *Holmes* v. *Jennison*, 14 Pet. (39 U.S.) 540, 614, 573 (1840).

[43] *Ibid.*, pp. 575-76.

[44] "I am . . . authorized by my brethren," says the Chief Justice, "to say, that, on an examination of the case, as decided by the supreme court of the United States, they think if the return had been as it now is, a majority of that court would have decided that Holmes was entitled to his discharge, and that the opinion of a majority of the supreme court of the United States was also adverse to the exercise of the power in question by any of the separate states of the union. The judgment of the court therefore is, that Holmes be discharged from his imprisonment." *Ex parte Holmes*, 12 Vt. 631, 642 (1840).

[45] 7 Pet. (32 U.S.) 243 (1833). [46] *Ibid.*, p. 249. [47] *Ibid.*

[48] See *supra*, Ch. II, pp. 27-30. The Court by way of dicta in the subsqeuent case of *United States* v. *Rauscher*, 119 U.S. 407, 414-15 (1886), reviewed *Holmes* v. *Jennison* and observed that "At this time of day, and after the repeated examinations which have been made by this court into the powers of the Federal government to deal with all such international questions exclusively, it can hardly be admitted that . . . the extradition of a fugitive from justice can become the subject of negotiation between a state of this Union and a foreign government. Fortunately, this question, with others which might arise in the absence of treaties or acts of Congress on the subject, is now of very little importance, since, with nearly all the nations of the world with whom our relations are such that fugitives from justice may be found within their dominions or within ours, we have treaties which govern the rights and conduct of the parties in such cases. These treaties are also supplemented by acts of Congress, and both are in their nature exclusive."

[49] See *supra*, Ch. II, p. 25. [50] 163 N.W. 540, 37 N.D. 59 (1917).

[51] *Ibid.*, p. 544. *Cf. Clark* v. *Allen*, 331 U.S. 503 (1947), where the Court sustained Section 259 of the California Probate Code as it existed in 1942 against the allegation that it was unconstitutional as an invasion by the State of the field of foreign affairs reserved to the Federal Government. The section in issue made the right of non-resident aliens to acquire personal property dependent upon the reciprocal rights of American citizens to do so in the countries of which the aliens were inhabitants or citizens, and, in the words of the Court, "Such an offer of reciprocal arrangements is said to be a matter for settlement by the Federal Government on a nation-wide basis." The Court pointed out that rights of succession to property are determined by local law, citing *Lyeth* v. *Hoey*, 305 U.S. 188, 193 (1938); *Irving Trust Co.* v. *Day*, 314 U.S. 556, 562 (1942). That determination, however, is "subject to overriding federal policy, as where a treaty makes different or conflicting arrangements. *Hauenstein* v. *Lynham*," 100 U.S. 483, 488-90 (1897). The Court pointed out that where such arrangements have

been made ". . . the state policy must give way. *Cf. Hines* v. *Davidowitz,* 312 U. S. 52 [1941]. But here there is no treaty governing the rights of succession to the personal property. Nor has California entered the forbidden domain of negotiating with a foreign country, *United States* v. *Curtiss-Wright Corp.,* 299 U.S. 304, 316-17 [1936], or making a compact with it contrary to the prohibition of Article I, Section 10 of the Constitution. What California has done will have some incidental or indirect effect in foreign countries. But that is true of many state laws which none would claim cross the forbidden line." 331 U.S. 503, 517 (1947).

[52] *McHenry County* v. *Brady,* 163 N.W. 540, 544, 37 N.D. 59 (1917). See *infra,* Ch. III, for cases in which state courts sustained on the basis of dicta in *Virginia* v. *Tennessee* interstate arrangements made without the consent of Congress.

[53] 153 U.S. 155 (1894). [54] *Ibid.,* p. 167.

[55] *Ibid.,* p. 168. [56] *Ibid.,* p. 170.

[57] *Ibid.,* p. 171. In *McCready* v. *Virginia,* 94 U.S. 391 (1876), the Supreme Court held that a State owns the beds of the tidewater lands within its jurisdiction and may set them aside for the common and exclusive use of its citizens in the cultivation of fish and fishing. Hence, a Virginia statute prohibiting the use of the State's tidewater beds for those activities by non-Virginians was upheld against contentions that it was in violation of the Privileges and Immunities and Commerce clauses of the Constitution. The Maryland-Virginia Compact was not considered.

[58] 11 Pet. (36 U.S.) 185 (1837).

[59] *Ibid.,* p. 209. An interesting and somewhat novel application of this statement is afforded by *Stearns* v. *Minnesota,* where the Court held binding upon Minnesota a "compact" formed by the enabling act by which Minnesota was admitted into the Union and by the Minnesota constitution. Mr. Justice Brewer, delivering the opinion of the Court, stated that "If as 'a part of the general right of sovereignty' to which Mr. Justice Story refers . . ., the right of agreement between one another belongs to the several States, except as limited by the constitutional provisions requiring the consent of Congress, equally true is it that a State may make a compact with all the States, constituting as one body the nation, possessed of general rights of sovereignty and represented by Congress." 179 U.S. 223, 248 (1900). But Mr. Justice Brewer continued: "In an inquiry as to the validity of such a compact this distinction must at the outset be noticed. There may be agreements or compacts attempted to be entered into between two States, or between a State and the nation, in reference to political rights and obligations, and there may be those solely in reference to property belonging to one or the other." *Ibid.,* p. 244. It is obvious that different considerations may enter into the question of the validity of the two types. "It has often been said that a State admitted into the Union enters therein in full equality with all the others, and such equality may forbid any agreement or compact limiting or qualifying political rights and obligations; whereas, on the other hand, a mere agreement in reference to property involves no question of equality of status, but only of the power of a State to deal with the nation or with any other State in reference to such property." *Ibid.,* p. 245. The case under consideration was "one involving simply an agreement as to property between a State and the nation."

[60] 12 Pet. (37 U.S.) 657 (1838).

[61] The case upon which the Court was called to pass is indicated in Mr. Justice

Baldwin's statement of the Rhode Island contention that the boundary line in issue was located too far to the south to Massachusetts' advantage and Rhode Island's disadvantage; that the agreements of 1710-1711, entered into between the two colonies for settlement of the boundary dispute were unfair and were executed under a misrepresentation and mistake as to material facts; that the line was not run according to the charters of the colonies; that the agreement was made without the assent of the King; that Massachusetts had continued to hold wrongful possession of the disputed territory, and prevented the exercise of the rightful jurisdiction and sovereignty of Rhode Island therein. The prayer of the bill was for settlement of the northern boundary between the States. *Ibid.*, p. 716. The present phase of the case, however, was concerned with the right of the Court to entertain jurisdiction of the bill as maintained by Rhode Island and denied by Massachusetts. This question of jurisdiction was the one primarily considered by counsel, albeit they treated the facts and merits of the case as well. The decree of the Court, as already indicated, was that it possessed jurisdiction and could entertain the controversy. The question was posed whether Massachusetts or Rhode Island were correct on the location of the starting point from which the charters prescribed that the line be drawn. If Massachusetts were right, the existent line was correct, and no legal foundation existed for the dispute. If Rhode Island were correct, the existing line was incorrect, unless the agreement between the colonies were valid and bound the States to that line.

[62] *Ibid.*, p. 725. [63] *Ibid.*

[64] *Ibid.*, p. 726. These words seem to lay the groundwork for the subsequent statement of the Court relative to the Constitution's Compact Clause in *Virginia* v. *Tennessee*, 148 U.S. 503, 519 (1893): "Looking at the clause in which the terms 'compact' or 'agreement' appear, it is evident that the prohibition is directed to the formation of any combination tending to the increase of political power in the States, which may encroach upon or interfere with the just supremacy of the United States."

[65] *Ibid.*, pp. 726-27. In the final determination of the case the Court pointed out that more than two centuries had elapsed since Massachusetts had claimed and taken possession of the territory in question, and continued: "This possession has ever since been steadily maintained, under an assertion of right. It would be difficult to disturb a claim thus sanctioned by time, however unfounded it might have been in its origin. . . . that right in the most solemn form has been admitted by the complainant . . . Forty years elapsed before a mistake was alleged, and since such allegation was made nearly a century has transpired. If in the agreements there was a departure from the strict construction of the charter, the commissioners of Rhode Island acted within their powers, for they were authorized 'to agree and settle the line between the said colonies in the best manner they can, as near agreeable to the royal charter as in honor they can compromise the same.'" Thus the Court held the agreement binding upon the States, deciding in favor of the Massachusetts claim. *Rhode Island* v. *Massachusetts,* 4 Howard (45 U.S.) 591, 638-39 (1846).

[66] 148 U.S. 503, 517 (1893). [67] *Ibid.*, p. 520. [68] *Ibid.*

[69] *Ibid. Cf.* the Court's statement in *Rhode Island* v. *Massachusetts, supra,* Ch. II, p. 35.

[70] *Virginia* v. *Tennessee,* 148 U.S. 503, 520 (1893). [71] *Ibid.*, p. 521.

[72] See *infra,* Ch. III, for treatment of the case in connection with congressional consent.

[73] See *supra*, Ch. II, pp. 25-26.

[74] 39 La. Ann. 447, 1 South. 822 (1887). See *infra*, Ch. III, for other examples of agreements sustained as not requiring the consent of Congress.

[75] "The great ordinances of the Constitution do not establish and divide fields of black and white. Even the more specific of them are found to terminate in a penumbra shading gradually from one extreme to the other." Mr. Justice Holmes dissenting in *Springer* v. *Phillippine Islands*, 277 U.S. 189, 209 (1928).

[76] *Fisher* v. *Steele*, 39 La. Ann. 447, 1 South, 882, 888 (1887).

[77] "No State shall . . . pass any . . . Law impairing the Obligation of Contracts. . . ." Article I, section 10, clause 1.

[78] 8 Wheat. (21 U.S.) 1 (1823). For background material on this case see Charles Warren, *The Supreme Court in United States History* (rev. edition; Boston: Little, Brown, and Company, 1947), I, Ch. XVI. It may be worthy of note that Professor Benjamin F. Wright observes that the Kentucky land case presented the Marshall Court's least important interpretation of the Contract Clause. "This holding that the clause protected interstate compacts had repercussions in the contemporary political opposition to the Court, but its legal effect was short-lived. Subsequent cases were dealt with, as this one should have been, under the clause permitting interstate compacts with the consent of Congress." *The Growth of American Constitutional Law* (Boston: Houghton Mifflin Company, 1942), p. 44. It would seem questionable whether the legal effect of the *Green* v. *Biddle* decision were short-lived, for, as will become apparent in subsequent cases, the Court has not overlooked the contractual character of interstate compacts.

[79] *Green* v. *Biddle*, 8 Wheat. (21 U.S.) 1, 91-92 (1823).

[80] *Ibid.*, p. 92. [81] 6 Cranch (10 U.S.) 87 (1810).

[82] *Green* v. *Biddle*, 8 Wheat. (21 U.S.) 1, 92-93 (1823).

[83] *Ibid.*, p. 106. Again it has been stated that "There are no technical words necessary to constitute a *compact*, or *contract*, which are convertible terms; and neither need be used, and seldom is, in the instrument creating it. It is a mutual consent of the minds of the parties concerned, respecting some property or right, that is the object of the stipulation, or something that is to be done or foreborne; 'a transaction between two or more persons, in which each party comes under an obligation to the other, and each reciprocally acquires a right to whatever is promised or stipulated by the other,' and any words manifesting that *congregatio mentium* are sufficient to constitute a contract." *Chesapeake & O. Canal Co.* v. *Baltimore & O. R. Co.*, Md., 4 Gill & J. 1, 129-130 (1832).

[84] *Green* v. *Biddle*, 8 Wheat. (21 U.S.) 1, 11 (1823).

[85] 5 Pet. (30 U.S.) 456 (1831). [86] *Ibid.*, pp. 465-66.

[87] 14 Pet. (39 U.S.) 540 (1840). See *supra*, Ch. II, for general treatment of case.

[88] *Ibid.*, p. 562. See *infra*, Ch. II, footnote 98, for text of the 25th section of the Judiciary Act of 1789.

[89] These four Justices held that this was not a case in which writ of error was given in the twenty-fifth section of the Judiciary Act because nothing appeared on the record warranting the conclusion that Vermont had authorized the Governor to exercise the power in question or that any arrangement had been made between Vermont and Canada on the subject (Mr. Justice Thompson, p. 581); the order to recommit, to bail, or discharge is not a final judgment or decree; the action of the Court is discretionary, depending on the nature of the case, the evidence,

and the usages of law, and no writ of error lies upon any proceeding in a cause depending on the discretion of the Court (Mr. Justice Baldwin, pp. 625-26); the agreement was not in the case to be upheld by the Vermont court and, hence, the arrest and decision in favor of its validity could not be repugnant to the federal Constitution (Mr. Justice Catron, p. 597); and the authority exercised by the Governor of Vermont was not in conflict with any federal treaty, statute, or provision of the federal Constitution, and consequently there is no ground for the clear and necessary intendment, or for any intendment that such matter was drawn in question, and decided by the court below, as is absolutely necessary to give this Court jurisdiction over a case brought from a state court (Mr. Justice Barbour, pp. 586-87).

[90] *United States* v. *Rauscher*, 119 U.S. 407, 414 (1886). See *supra*, Ch. II, p. 57, footnote 48.

[91] *Ibid.*, p. 415. [92] 13 How. (54 U.S.) 518 (1851).

[93] *Cf. Missouri* v. *Illinois*, 200 U.S. 496, 519 (1906).

[94] *Pennsylvania* v. *Wheeling and Belmont Bridge Co.*, 18 How. (59 U.S.) 421, 430 (1855).

[95] Thus the Court refused complainant's motions for a writ of assistance to execute the decree of the Court in the first *Wheeling Bridge* case by the abatement of the bridge and for a sequestration against the corporation and attachment against its officers for disobeying that decree. "So far, therefore, as this bridge created an obstruction to the free navigation of the river, in view of the previous acts of congress, they are to be regarded as modified by this subsequent legislation; and, although it still may be an obstruction in fact, is not so in the contemplation of law. We have already said, and the principle is undoubted, that the act of the legislature of Virginia conferred full authority to erect and maintain the bridge, subject to the exercise of the power of congress to regulate the navigation of the river. That body having in the exercise of this power, regulated the navigation consistent with its preservation and continuation, the authority to maintain it would seem to be complete. That authority combines the concurrent powers of both governments, state and federal, which, if not sufficient, certainly none can be found in our system of government." *Ibid.*

[96] 12 Wall. (79 U.S.) 455 (1870). [97] *Ibid.*, p. 456.

[98] *Ibid.* The "25th section of the Judiciary Act" of 1789 provides "That a final judgment or decree in any suit, in the highest court of law or equity of a State in which a decision in the suit could be had, where is drawn in question the validity of a treaty or statute of, or an authority, exercised under the United States, and the decision is against their validity; or where is drawn in question the validity of a statute of, or an authority exercised under any State, on the ground of their being repugnant to the constitution, treaties or laws of the United States, and the decision is in favour of such their validity, or where is drawn in question the construction of any clause of the constitution, or of a treaty, or statute of, or commission held under the United States, and the decision is against the title, right, privilege or exemption specially set up or claimed by either party, under such clause of the said Constitution, treaty, statute or commission, may be re-examined and reversed or affirmed in the Supreme Court of the United States upon a writ of error. . . ." 1 United States *Statutes at Large* 85-86.

[99] *Cf. Hamburg American Steamship Co.* v. *Grube*, 196 U.S. 407 (1905), where the Court flatly rejected a contention that it possessed jurisdiction in a case arising under the New York-New Jersey compact of 1833 because of the

act of Congress giving consent to the agreement. The Court stated that the "proposition raised no Federal question." *Ibid.*, p. 413. The Court entertained jurisdiction in the case, but on another ground. Rejection of the first contention was in accord with the course of action followed by the Court in *People* v. *Central Railroad.*

[100] 219 U.S. 140 (1911). [101] *Ibid.*, p. 161. [102] See *supra*, Ch. II.

[103] 281 U.S. 163 (1930). [104] *Ibid.*, p. 173. [105] *Ibid.*, p. 165.

[106] 246 U.S. 289 (1918). The Court reversed the Tennessee judgment to which reference is made in *Arkansas* v. *Tennessee*, 246 U.S. 158 (1918).

[107] The Tennessee court held that the location of the western boundary of the State of Tennessee depended upon the interpretation of the Treaty of 1783 between the United States and Great Britain, the act of cession from North Carolina to the United States made in 1790, the Treaty of 1795 between the United States and Spain, the Act of Congress of June 1, 1796, admitting Tennessee into the Union as a State, the Louisiana Purchase Treaty of 1803, and the Act of Congress of June 15, 1836, admitting Arkansas as a State *Cissna* v. *Tennessee*, 246 U.S. 289, 294 (1918).

[108] *Ibid.*, p. 295.

[109] 11 Wall. (78 U.S.) 39 (1870). See *infra*, Ch. IV, for treatment of this case.

[110] *Ibid.*, p. 53. [111] *Ibid.*, p. 55.

[112] 192 U.S. 573 (1904). This was a writ of error to the Circuit Court of the State of Kentucky on a judgment entered there in pursuance of a mandate of the state Court of Appeals. Action was brought upon an Indiana judgment, and the answer denied the Indiana court's jurisdiction. In the words of Mr. Justice Holmes, who stated the facts of the case prior to delivery of the opinion of the Court, "At the trial two questions were left to the jury, one whether the person purporting to act as the attorney of the defendant in the Indiana suit was authorized to represent him, and the other whether the summons in that suit was served on the Indiana or Kentucky side of the low-water mark of the Ohio River where it touches the Indiana shore." Service was on a steamboat in the Ohio River. "The jury found against the authority of the alleged attorney, and found that the service was on the Kentucky side of the low-water mark, and therefore, it is assumed, within the boundaries of Kentucky. Thereupon the plaintiffs in error (the original plaintiffs) moved for judgment notwithstanding the findings of the jury, and judgment was ordered. The defendant excepted and appealed. The Court of Appeals sustained the exceptions and ordered a judgment on the verdict dismissing the action. A judgment was entered, as ordered, in the court below, the above mentioned Circuit Court, and this writ of error was brought." *Ibid.*, pp. 580-81.

[113] 304 U. S. 92 (1938). This was an appeal from the affirmance by the Colorado State Court of a judgment requiring water officials of Colorado to permit diversion of water for irrigation from the La Plata River by the La Plata River and Cherry Creek Ditch Company, in spite of provisions to the contrary in the La Plata River Compact. Appeal was dismissed, certiorari granted. The Supreme Court decision reversed the holding of the state court.

[114] *Ibid.*, p. 109. Section 237 (a) of the Judicial Code provides that "A final judgment or decree in any suit in the highest court of a State in which a decision in the suit could be had, where is drawn in question the validity of a treaty or

statute of the United States, and the decision is against its validity; or where is drawn, in question the validity of a statute of any State, on the ground of its being repugnant to the Constitution, treaties, or laws of the United States, and the decision is in favor of its validity, may be reviewed by the Supreme Court upon a writ of error. The writ shall have the same effect as if the judgment or decree had been rendered or passed in a court of the United States. The Supreme Court may reverse, modify, or affirm the judgment or decree of such State court, and may, in its discretion, award execution or remand the cause to the court from which it was removed by the writ." *Cf.* 25th Section of the Judiciary Act of 1789, *supra,* Ch. II, footnote 98.

[115] See *infra,* Ch. II, footnote 124, for extract from Section 237 (b) of the Judicial Code.

[116] *Hinderlider* v. *La Plata Co.,* 304 U.S. 92, 110 (1938). Mr. Justice Brandeis' allusion to "federal common law" is rather surprising in view of the fact that he wrote the opinion of the Court in *Erie Railroad Co.* v. *Tompkins,* 304 U.S. 64 (1938), overruling *Swift* v. *Tyson,* 16 Pet. (41 U.S.) 1 (1842), and that decision was handed down on the same day as the one in the *Hinderlider* case. In the *Erie Railroad Company* case Mr. Justice Brandeis quoted approvingly Mr. Justice Holmes' dissenting opinion in *Kuhn* v. *Fairmont Coal Company,* 215 U.S. 349, 370-72 (1910), stating: "The fallacy underlying the rule declared in *Swift* v. *Tyson* is made clear by Mr. Justice Holmes. The doctrine rests upon the assumption that there is 'a transcendental body of law outside of any particular State but obligatory within it unless and until changed by statute'; that federal courts have the power to use their judgment as to what the rules of common law are; and that in the federal courts 'the parties are entitled to an independent judgment on matters of general law': 'but law in the sense in which courts speak of it today does not exist without some definite authority behind it. The common law so far as it is enforced in a State, whether called common law or not, is not the common law generally but the law of that State existing by the authority of that State without regard to what it may have been in England or anywhere else. . . . the authority and only authority is the State, and if that be so, the voice adopted by the State as its own [whether it be of its Legislature or of its Supreme Court] should utter the last word.' Thus the doctrine of *Swift* v. *Tyson* is, as Mr. Justice Holmes said, 'an unconstitutional assumption of powers by courts of the United States which no lapse of time or respectable array of opinion should make us hesitate to correct'." *Erie Railroad Co.* v. *Tompkins,* 304 U.S. 64, 79 (1938).

[117] *Hinderlider* v. *La Plata Co.,* 304 U.S. 92, 110 (1938).

[118] It was also pointed out that in *Howard* v. *Ingersoll,* 13 How. (54 U.S.) 381 (1851), the Court reversed the Supreme Court of Alabama's decision locating the Alabama-Georgia boundary, which depended upon the construction of a cession of territory by Georgia to the United States in 1802. *Hinderlider* v. *La Plata Co.,* 304 U.S. 92, 110, note 12 (1938); *cf. Coffee* v. *Groover,* 123 U.S. 1 (1887).

[119] *Hinderlider* v. *La Plata Co.,* 304 U.S. 92, 110, note 12 (1938). As to the lack of uniformity in decisions on whether the interpretation of a compact presents a federal question, the Court points to a comparison of *People* v. *Central Railroad,* 12 Wall. (79 U.S.) 455 (1870), on the one hand, and *Wedding* v. *Meyler,* 192 U.S. 573 (1904), and *Wharton* v. *Wise,* 153 U.S. 155 (1894), all

considered above, on the other. This matter was again subjected to scrutiny by the Court in the case considered immediately below.

[120] 310 U.S. 419 (1940). This case was a proceeding in mandamus brought in the New Jersey Supreme Court to compel the Delaware River Joint Toll Bridge Commission, a "body corporate and politic" created by the compact of 1934 between New Jersey and Pennsylvania and authorized to build bridges over the Delaware River, to fix and award compensation to respondents for damages to their land suffered by reason of the Commission's construction of a bridge abutment adjacent to it. The New Jersey Supreme Court sustained the special verdict of a jury which found the action deprived the respondents of "access to their land and their enjoyment of light, air and view." A New Jersey statute was held applicable and authority for recovery. The court awarded a peremptory mandamus. On appeal the New Jersey Court of Errors and Appeals affirmed. The Supreme Court granted certiorari. Deciding that the compact of 1934 excluded the application of the New Jersey statute to the Commission, without which the respondents would enjoy no right of recovery under New Jersey law, the Court reversed the state court's decision.

[121] *Ibid.*, p. 427. See *Delaware River Joint Toll Bridge Commission* v. *Colburn,* 308 U.S. 549 (1940).

[122] *Delaware River Joint Toll Bridge Commission* v. *Colburn,* 310 U.S. 419, 427 (1940).

[123] 304 U.S. 92, 110, note 12 (1938).

[124] *Delaware River Joint Toll Bridge Commission* v. *Colburn,* 310 U.S. 419, 427 (1940). The pertinent provision of Section 237 (b) of the Judicial Code runs as follows: "It shall be competent for the Supreme Court, by certiorari, to require that there be certified to it for review and determination, with the same power and authority and with like effect as if brought up by writ of error, any cause wherein a final judgment or decree has been rendered or passed by the highest court of a State in which a decision could be had . . . where any title, right, privilege, or immunity is specially set up or claimed by either party under the Constitution, or any treaty or statute of, or commission held or authority exercised under, the United States; and the power to review under this paragraph may be exercised as well where the Federal claim is sustained as where it is denied."

[125] 341 U.S. 22 (1951).

[126] West Virginia along with seven other States entered the Ohio River Valley Water Sanitation Compact for the control of pollution in the Ohio River system. See *infra,* Ch. V, for a treatment of this compact as one of the uses to which the Compact Clause has been put. The Compact, which became operative in 1948, provided for establishment of a Commission empowered to administer its provisions and stipulated that the expenses of the Commission should be shared by the signatory States. The West Virginia auditor, Sims, refused to issue a warrant upon the state treasury for payment of the legislative appropriation made in 1949 to meet the West Virginia share of the expenses for that fiscal year. A mandamus action was then brought in the Supreme Court of Appeals of West Virginia to compel issuance of the warrant. That court sustained the auditor's refusal, invalidating the 1939 West Virginia act ratifying the compact, on the grounds that the act delegated West Virginia's police power to other States and to the Federal Government and that it bound future legislatures to make appropriations for the continued activities of the Commission in a fashion violative of the state constitu-

tion's debt limitation provision. Article X, section 4 of the West Virginia constitution stipulates that "No debt shall be contracted by this State, except to meet casual deficits in revenue, to redeem a previous liability of the State, to suppress insurrection, repel invasion or defend the State in time of war; but the payment of any liability other than that for the ordinary expenses of the State, shall be equally distributed over a period of at least twenty years." The United States Supreme Court granted certiorari [*West Virginia ex rel Dyer* v. *Sims,* 340 U.S. 807 (1950)] and reversed the decision of the West Virginia court with respect to invalidity. *Ibid.,* 341 U.S. 22 (1951). The Court pointed out that each State was represented on the Commission by three Commissioners and that no commission order went into effect under the provisions of the Compact "unless and until it receives the assent of at least a majority of the commissioners from each of not less than a majority of the signatory States," and no such order upon a municipality, corporation, person or entity in any State went into effect "unless and until it receives the assent of not less than a majority of the commissioners from such State." Article IX, 341 U.S. 22, 25 (1951). Moreover, under Article X of the Compact, the States agreed to appropriate "their proper proportion of the annual budget as determined by the Commission and approved by the Governors of the signatory States." On neither count was the West Virginia act held beyond its constitutional power. With respect to the delegation of power to an interstate agency the Court thought what was involved only the "conventional grant of legislative power." There was nothing indicative that West Virginia might not solve "a problem such as the control of river pollution by compact and by the delegation, if such it be, necessary to effectuate such solution by compact." 341 U.S. 22, 31 (1951). With respect to the second item, violation of the state constitution's debt limitation clause, the Court said that the compact was obviously carefully drawn to meet the problem of debt limitation in the light of the West Virginia and other State's restrictive constitutional provisions. Hence the Commission's annual budget was made subject to approval by the Governors of the signatory States, and no obligations were to be incurred by the Commission according to Article V of the Compact until the "making of appropriations adequate to meet the same," nor was the credit of any of the signatory States to be pledged "except by and with the authority of the legislature thereof." *Ibid.,* p. 32. The Court concluded "in view of these provisions" that the obligation of the State under the Compact was not in conflict with the state constitution's debt limitation provision. In the process of answering these points the Court of course was exercising jurisdiction and that point is the significant one in the above connection.

[127] *Ibid.,* p. 28 [128] *Ibid.,* [129] *Ibid.,* p. 29. See *supra,* pp. 44-45.

[130] See *supra,* pp. 46-47.

[131] *West Virginia ex rel. Dyer* v. *Sims,* 341 U.S. 22, 30 (1951).

[132] *Ibid.,* p. 26. [133] Story, *op. cit.,* II, 310. [134] 148 U.S. 503, 519 (1893).

[135] 14 Pet. (39 U.S.) 540, 572 (1840).

[136] *Wharton* v. *Wise,* 153 U.S. 155, 171 (1894).

[137] 11 Pet. (36 U.S.) 185, 209 (1837). [138] 179 U.S. 223, 248 (1900).

[139] The opinion of Mr. Justice Brewer, who spoke for the Court in that case, might be interpreted as making an admission as to the nature of the Union which would validate the stand taken by the States of Kentucky and Virginia in their resolutions of 1798. The Virginia Resolution resolved in part "That this Assembly doth explicitly and peremptorily declare, that it views the powers of the federal

government as resulting from the compact to which the states are parties. . . ." Elliot, *op. cit.*, IV, 528.

[140] 8 Wheat. (21 U.S.) 1, 92 (1823). [141] *Ibid.*, p. 106. [142] *Ibid.*, p. 88.

[143] 5 Pet (30 U.S.) 456, 466-67 (1831). [144] 14 Pet. (39 U.S.) 540, 562 (1840).

[145] *Pennsylvania* v. *Wheeling and Belmont Bridge Co.*, 13 How. (54 U.S.) 518, 566 (1851).

[146] See "Some Legal and Practical Problems of the Interstate Compact." *Yale Law Journal*, 45:328, December, 1935; "Legal Problems Relating to Interstate Compacts." *Iowa Law Review*, 23:628, May, 1938.

[147] 281 U.S. 163, 165 (1930). [148] 12 Wall. (79 U.S.) 455, 456 (1870).

[149] 281 U.S. 163, 176 (1930). [150] 246 U.S. 289, 295 (1918).

[151] *Hinderlider* v. *La Plata Co.*, 304 U.S. 92, 109 (1938).

[152] 310 U.S. 419, 427 (1940). [153] 341 U.S. 22, 30 (1951).

Chapter III

CONGRESSIONAL CONSENT

The considerations underlying the congressional consent requirement in the provision that "No State shall, without the consent of Congress, . . . enter into any agreement or compact with another State, or with a foreign power. . . ." have been treated above.[1] But what have been the developments in connection with the consent element in the cases which have come before the courts? It has frequently been contended before the courts that a given compact was invalid because made without the consent of Congress. The opinions of the courts in these cases have clarified many points relative to the consent requirement.

The part-whole relationship underlying the constitutional requirement of congressional consent for interstate agreements was considered in the case of *Florida* v. *Georgia,*[2] where the Court held that the relationship warranted granting the Attorney-General leave to be heard on behalf of the United States in the boundary suit between the States of Florida and Georgia. Though the case presented a suit between two States as to the true boundary line between them, the other States in the Union, "whose interests are represented by the United States," were also deemed interested in the adjustment of the boundary, for their interests might "be different from those of either of the litigating states."[3] In fact, the Court thought that unless the United States could be heard in some form or other in the suit, "one of the great safeguards of the Union, provided in the constitution, would in effect be annulled."[4] The safeguard alluded to is the provision that no State may enter into any agreement or compact with another State without the consent of Congress. The Court noted that a question of boundary between States was in its nature a political question to be settled by compact made by the political department of the government, and, if Florida and Georgia were to proceed by negotiation and agreement to adjust their boundary, any compact between them would be null and void without the assent of Congress. The obvious intention of the provision requiring that assent was to guard the rights and interests of the other States, and to prevent any compact or agreement between any two States which might affect injuriously the interests of the others. And the duty to protect those interests was vested in the general government. But under the American governmental system an interstate boundary when it becomes the subject of a controversy between States becomes a judicial question to be decided in the Supreme Court, and, when it assumes that form, the assent or disapproval of the United States cannot influence the decision. The question is to be decided upon the evidence brought before the Court; and that decision, when pronounced, is conclusive upon the United States, as well as upon the States that are parties to the suit.

As it is made the duty of the United States by the Constitution to examine into the subject in a case of compact and to determine whether or not the boundary proposed by the agreement is consistent with the interests of the other States of the Union, it would seem to be equally their duty to watch over these interests when they are in litigation in the Court and about to be decided. And the duty of the United States would seem to presuppose a corresponding right to adduce evidence and be heard before judgment is given. This is the only manner in which the United States can guard the interests of the rest of the Union when the boundary dispute is settled by suit. If it were otherwise, the litigating States might "by admissions of facts and by agreements admitting or rejecting testimony, place a case before the court which would necessarily be decided according to their wishes,"[5] excluding from the consideration of the Court the interest and rights of the rest of the Union. The States might thus, in the form of an action, accomplish what the Constitution prohibits their doing directly by compact. Entrance of the United States into such cases merely carries into effect a provision of the Constitution adopted by the States for their general safety and "maintains that universal principle of justice and equity, which gives to every party, whose interest will be affected by the judgment, the right to be heard."[6] Thus the Attorney-General, the Court held, has a right to appear on behalf of the United States, to present proofs in support of the boundary it deems correct, and to be heard in the argument. The United States does not become a party in the technical sense, and judgment is not rendered for it, but arguments and evidence advanced in its behalf are to be considered by the Court in reaching its decision on the matter in controversy.

The Court in this case points directly to the considerations underlying the consent requirement for compacts involving interstate boundaries. Also it throws light on the fact that this same set of considerations is involved in a boundary suit between States. The problem of safeguarding the interests of the whole through control of the actions of its parts remains. The case not only presents an interesting inference from the Compact Clause, but also indicates that the restriction of power of agreement among the States would fail to safeguard the interests of the whole if other avenues of injury remained.

The consent element of the Compact Clause has been considered by the courts in several cases, and several questions with respect to it have been laid to rest. Thus it has been held that Congress alone decides the mode or form in which it is to signify its consent; that consent need not be express but may be inferred from circumstances, indeed may be implied from subsequent congressional legislation and proceedings; that the consent of Congress to an agreement is sufficiently indicated by the adoption or approval of proceedings taken under it; and that Congress may stipulate conditions upon which its consent will be granted. Moreover, in obiter dicta in Supreme Court opinions and in state court decisions it has been indicated that consent may not be necessary at all for agreements upon matters which in no respect concern the United States.[7]

The principle that Congress is the proper judge as to when and how its consent is to be given to interstate agreements emerged from the case of *Green* v. *Biddle*,[8] in which it was contended that the Virginia-Kentucky compact of 1789 was invalid because in violation of the requirement prescribed in the Compact Clause of the Constitution in that it was made without the consent of Congress. The Court pointed out "that the constitution makes no provision respecting the mode or form in which the consent of congress is to be signified, very properly leaving the matter to the wisdom of that body, to be decided upon according to the ordinary rules of law, and of right reason."[9] Though the question arises as to what constitutes "right reason," there is no doubt that Congress is the proper body, according to the Court, to decide how its consent is to be given to interstate compacts. Congress passed an act with respect to the Virginia-Kentucky compact, which, after referring to the compact, consented to the creation of the "separate and independent state" of Kentucky and provided for her reception into the Union. The Court observed that Congress, although it could have refused its consent to the separation, was without authority to declare Kentucky a separate and independent State without Virginia's assent or upon terms other than those prescribed by Virginia. But after recognizing the conditions upon which Virginia agreed to the separation, Congress expressed by a solemn act the consent of that body to the separation. The terms and conditions, then, on which alone the separation could take place, or the act of Congress become a valid one, were necessarily assented to, "not by a mere tacit acquiescence, but by an express declaration of the legislative mind, resulting from the manifest construction of the act itself."[10] Mr. Justice Washington, speaking for the Court, admonished Kentucky counsel: "To deny this, is to deny the validity of the act of congress, without which, Kentucky could not have become an independent state; and then it would follow, that she is, at this moment, a part of the state of Virginia, and all her laws are acts of usurpation. The counsel who urged this argument," he continued, "would not, we are persuaded, consent to this conclusion; and yet it would seem to be inevitable, if the premises insisted upon be true." [11]

The Court has held that the consent of Congress need not be express but may be inferred from circumstances. This principle emerged from the decision of the Court in *Virginia* v. *West Virginia*, [12] a case arising out of the Virginia-West Virginia compact. The Court was called upon to settle the boundary line between the States, more particularly to decide whether the counties of Berkeley and Jefferson belonged to Virginia or West Virginia. Virginia brought action seeking a judgment that those counties properly belonged to her, advancing several grounds in support of such a judgment. Among other things, Virginia contended that a vote of the residents of the two counties had not been taken so as to satisfy the requirement stipulated by the constitution of the new State and the act of consent adopted by the "restored government" of Virginia, and that the "restored government" of Virginia had withdrawn its consent as to the transfer of the counties in issue before the agreement was consummated. The Court rejected Virginia's contentions, declaring that the Virginia Governor's certificate to the effect that a vote in the counties favored transfer was binding upon the Court. On this ground the West Virginia claim to the two counties was sustained. [13] In so holding the Court considered three questions:

"1. Did the State of Virginia ever give a consent to this proposition which became obligatory on her?

"2. Did the Congress give such consent as rendered the agreement valid?

"3. If both these are answered affirmatively, it may be necessary to inquire whether the circumstances alleged in this bill, authorized Virginia to withdraw her consent, and justify us in setting aside the contract, and restoring the two counties to that State." [14]

It was held with respect to the first question that the two States had entered into an agreement to the effect that the two counties should become a part of West Virginia. The Court observed that there was one condition, however, imposed by Virginia to her parting with them, and one condition made by West Virginia to her receiving them, and that was the same—namely, the assent of the majority of the voters of the counties to the transfer.

The Court then proceeded to consider whether Congress consented to the agreement, prefacing its inquiry with the observation that "Unless it can be shown that the consent of Congress, under that clause of the Constitution which forbids agreements between States without it, can only be given in the form of an express and formal statement of every proposition of the agreement, and of its consent thereto, we must hold that the consent of that body was given to this agreement."[15] The Court noted that the attention of Congress was called to the subject by the short Virginia statute requesting the admission of the new State into the Union. One of the three sections of this statute was entirely devoted to giving consent that these two counties and the county of Frederick might become a part of West Virginia, if they desired to do so. Moreover, the constitution of the new State was literally cumbered with the various provisions for receiving these counties if they chose to come, and in two or three forms express consent was there given to this addition to the State.[16] The Court asserted that the subject of the relation of these counties to the others, as set forth in the ordinance for calling the convention, in the constitution framed by that convention, and in the act of the Virginia legislature, must have received the attentive consideration of Congress. To hold otherwise would be to suppose that the act for the admission of the new State passed without due or serious consideration. The Court rejected this supposition, observing that, if any part of the constitution had failed to meet the approbation of Congress, especially so important a part as the proposition for a future change of boundary between the new and the old States, it was reasonable to suppose that its dissent would have been expressed in some shape, especially as the refusal to permit those counties to attach themselves to the new State would not have endangered the formation and admission of the State without them. The Court concluded that it is an "inference clear and satisfactory" that Congress by the statute admitting the new State into the Union intended to consent to the admission of the State with the contingent boundaries provided for in its constitution and in the statute of Virginia, and that in so doing it necessarily consented to the agreement of those States on that subject. There was, then, a valid agreement between the two States consented to by Congress which made the accession of these counties dependent on the result of a popular vote in favor of that proposition.

The Virginia contention that no such vote was ever taken in the counties the Court rejected, holding the action of the Virginia Governor, certifying to West Virginia that the vote was taken and was in favor of transfer, to be "conclusive of the vote as between the States of Virginia and West Virginia."[17] The Court observed that its view of this subject rendered it unnecessary to inquire into the effect of the Virginia act withdrawing that State's consent to the transfer or the effect of a joint resolution of Congress of 1866 giving the consent of Congress to the transfer of the counties of Berkeley and Jefferson to the State of West Virginia after Virginia's attempt to withdraw her consent.[18]

Thus the consent the Constitution requires as to valid agreements under the Compact Clause is not necessarily to be an expressed consent but may be inferred from circumstances.[19] But what are the circumstances from which it may be inferred? The Court in the case below pointed out that Congress by adopting the results of an agreement and using them for the basis of legislation signified its consent to the agreement.

In *Virginia* v. *Tennessee*,[20] the Court again considered the element of congressional consent, liberally interpreting the requirement that no compact be made without such consent. It said that the Constitution does not state when the consent of Congress shall be given, whether it shall precede or may follow the making of the compact, or whether it shall be express or may be implied. The Court noted that in many cases consent will usually precede the compact or agreement, "as where it is to lay a duty of tonnage, to keep troops or ships of war in time of peace, or to engage in war."[21] But where the agreement relates to a matter which could not well be considered until its nature is fully developed, consent may be given subsequently. The Court hearkened back to Story, noting that the consent of Congress may be implied and is always to be implied when Congress adopts the particular act by sanctioning its objects and aiding in enforcing them; and that, where a State is admitted into the Union upon the terms of a compact made between it and the State of which it previously was a part, the act of Congress admitting such State into the Union is an implied consent to the terms of the compact. "Knowledge by Congress of the boundaries of a State, and of its political subdivisions, may reasonably be presumed, as much of its legislation is affected by them, such as relates to the territorial jurisdiction of the courts of the United States, the extent of their collection districts, and of districts in which process, civil and criminal, of their courts may be served and enforced."[22] In the case of the Virginia-Tennessee boundary agreement, the Court indicated that the consent of Congress could not have preceded the execution of the compact, for, until the line was run, it could not be known where it would lie and whether or not it would receive the approval of the States. The preliminary agreement was not to accept a line run, whatever it might be, but to receive from the designated commissioners a report as to the line which might be run and established by them. Each State was free to take whatever action it saw fit on that report. Congressional approval of the compact entered into between the States upon their ratification of the action of their commissioners was fairly to be implied from subsequent legislation and proceedings of Congress. The line established was treated by that body as the true boundary between the States in the assignment of territory north of it as a portion of districts set apart for judicial and revenue purposes in Virginia, and as included in territory in which federal elections were to be held, and for which appointments were to be made by federal authority in that State. Similarly the territory south of the boundary was treated as a portion of Tennessee.[23] The Court indicated that "Such use of the territory on different sides of the boundary designated, in a single instance would not, perhaps, be considered as absolute proof of the assent or approval of Congress to the boundary line; but the exercise of jurisdiction by Congress over the country as a part of Tennessee on one side, and as a part of Virginia on the other, for a long succession of years, without question or dispute from any quarter, furnishes as conclusive proof of assent to it by that body as can usually be obtained from its most formal proceedings."[24]

Also in the case of *Virginia* v. *Tennessee* the Court, as has already been indicated, intimated that there are many matters upon which different States may agree that can in no respect concern the United States and for which it would not be necessary to obtain the consent of Congress.[25]

The Court clarified somewhat the confusion created by this intimation by noting that the prohibition is directed to the formation of any combination tending to the increase of political power in the States, which might encroach upon or interfere with the just supremacy of the United States. This distinction seems to introduce the "political" element as a distinctive characteristic, the presence of which in an agreement makes necessary the grant of congressional consent for its validity, and the absence of which renders such consent unnecessary.

The suggestion that States may make "compacts" or "agreements" without the consent of Congress and the doctrine of implied consent have been subjected to severe criticism albeit not judicial criticism. Thus the doctrine of implied consent has been called the "doubtful doctrine of implied consent,"[26] and it has been said with respect to the intimation that agreements may be made without congressional consent that it would be better to admit that the plain words of the Constitution mean what they say, and that every agreement or compact between the States requires for its validity the consent of Congress.[27] The

Virginia v. *Tennessee* holding would seem to invalidate completely the adjective "doubtful" as applied to the doctrine of implied consent. Moreover, the Court in case after case repeated the dicta as to compacts or agreements without the consent of Congress laid down in *Virginia* v. *Tennessee,*[28] rendering the contention that every agreement or compact between the States requires for its validity the consent of Congress debatable. After all, as Charles Evans Hughes once said: "We are under a Constitution, but the Constitution is what the judges say it is. . . ."[29]

The dicta of the Supreme Court with regard to arrangements not requiring congressional consent have support, moreover, in numerous state court decisions and dicta. State courts have sustained agreements made without the consent of Congress between a local governmental division of North Dakota and the local government unit opposite it in Canada for the construction of a drain for the removal of surface waters;[30] between States for the construction of a bridge over an interstate river;[31] between States for cooperative action in connection with the construction of an interstate railroad;[32] and between States for the construction of a levee for the protection of land subject to flood.[33]

Conditional Consent. Yet another point worthy of consideration in connection with consent is whether Congress may influence the substance of an interstate agreement in granting its approval. Expressed somewhat differently, this question concerns the nature of the power conferred upon Congress by the words "without the consent of Congress." Is the congressional power one merely of granting or withholding its assent to interstate agreements, or may Congress condition its consent upon modification of the agreement which is tendered for its approval? The answer of the Court is that the power to consent includes the power to stipulate conditions upon which consent will be granted.

In dealing with the consent of Congress to a non-discriminatory state tax upon the gross receipts of a contractor engaged in dam construction for the Federal Government, the Court stated that "Normally, where governmental consent is essential, the consent may be granted upon terms appropriate to the subject and transgressing no constitutional limitation."[34] Using the Compact Clause as an example, Chief Justice Hughes, speaking for the Court, observed that the Constitution provides that no State without the consent of Congress shall enter into a compact with another State. "It can hardly be doubted that in giving consent Congress may impose conditions."[35]

An example of the imposition of conditions upon which congressional consent was made contingent is afforded by the Act of Congress of December 21, 1928, known as the Boulder Canyon Project Act.[36] This Act approved the Colorado River Compact subject to certain limitations and conditions, the approval to become effective upon the ratification of the compact, *as so modified,* by California and at least five of the other six States.

Section 19 of the Act also affords an interesting example of consent-in-advance to enter agreements and provision for subsequent ratification of those agreements. That section grants the consent of Congress to the States of Arizona, California, Colorado, Nevada, New Mexico, Utah, and Wyoming to negotiate and enter into compacts or agreements supplemental to and in conformity with the Colorado River compact. Consent, however, is "given upon condition that a representative of the United States, to be appointed by the President, shall participate in the negotiations and shall make report to Congress of the proceedings and of any compact or agreement entered into." The section further provides that "No such compact or agreement shall be binding or obligatory upon any of such States unless and until it has been approved by the legislature of each of such States and by the Congress of the United States."[37]

The provision that "No such compact or agreement shall be binding or obligatory upon any of such States" until approved emphasizes the contractual character of an interstate compact and leads naturally to questions concerning the enforcement of such a compact. These questions will be considered below.

Summary. The cases treated in this section indicate a relaxation in the application of the requirement of congressional consent for interstate compacts. Consent need not be express but may reasonably be implied. If express, it may be given before or after the agreement; and Congress is the proper judge as to when and how its consent should be given. Presumably, however, prior consent is not meant as a substitute for subsequent approval. In practice, it is merely an invitation to negotiate. The congressional power to consent includes the power to stipulate conditions upon which consent will be granted. Dicta in Supreme Court cases and state court decisions indicate that consent need not be given at all to interstate agreements in connection with many matters that can in no respect concern the United States. The direction in which the Court is moving seems to be indicated fairly well. Whether that direction is altogether desirable is a debatable point. The extreme statements of Ernest J. Carman,[38] who advocates elimination of the consent requirement for such compacts, might well be weighed against considerations such as that indicated in the following critical comment on the trend: "The practice of permitting some agreements to be made without Congressional consent may be criticized on the ground that the potentialities of an interstate bargain of apparently innocuous nature may thus escape Congressional attention."[39]

[1] See *supra,* Ch. I. [2] 17 How. (58 U.S.) 478 (1854).

[3] *Ibid.,* p. 494. [4] *Ibid.* [5] *Ibid.,* p. 495. [6] *Ibid.*

[7] *Virginia* v. *Tennessee,* 148 U.S. 503 (1893); *McHenry County* v. *Brady,* 163 N.W. 540, 37 N.D. 59 (1917); *Dover* v. *Portsmouth Bridge,* 17 N.H. 200 (1845); *Union Branch Rail Road Co.* v. *East Tennessee and Georgia R. R. Co.,* 14 Ga. 327 (1853); and *Fisher* v. *Steele,* 39 La. Ann. 447, 1 South. 882 (1887).

[8] 8 Wheat. (21 U.S.) 1 (1823). See *supra,* Ch. II, for treatment of other aspects of this case.

[9] *Ibid.,* pp. 85-86. [10] *Ibid.,* p. 87. [11] *Ibid.*

[12] 11 Wall. (78 U.S.) 39 (1870).

[13] James Garfield Randall points out that, in the absence of any decision on the legality of the creative process by which the new State was brought into existence, the instant case was more significant for what it assumed than for what it decided. West Virginia's legal existence was assumed without question. As Randall puts it, "In sum, this case, with its decision in favor of West Virginia, amounts to an admission by the old State and an affirmation by the Supreme Court that the proceedings concerning the partition of Virginia were valid. The whole controversy as to which one of the States possessed the two counties would obviously have been without significance if this validity had not been conceded." James G. Randall, *Constitutional Problems under Lincoln* (New York: D. Appleton and Company, 1926), pp. 470-71. For treatment of the partitioning of Virginia see *ibid.,* Ch. XVIII and works there cited.

[14] *Virginia* v. *West Virginia,* 11 Wall. (78 U.S.) 39, 56 (1870).

[15] *Ibid.,* p. 59.

[16] *Ibid.,* p. 60. The pertinent section of the Virginia statute runs as follows: "That the consent of the legislature of Virginia be, and the same is hereby given, that the counties of *Berkeley, Jefferson,* and *Frederick,* shall be included in and form part of the State of West Virginia WHENEVER the voters of said counties shall ratify and assent to the said constitution, at an election held for the purpose, at such time and under such regulations as the commissioners named in the said schedule may prescribe." *Ibid.,* p. 43.

[17] *Ibid.,* p. 62.

[18] *Ibid.,* p. 49. Justices Davis, Clifford, and Field, dissenting, deemed Virginia's withdrawal of her consent prior to congressional action on the transfer sufficient to render congressional action of no import. "There is no difference of opinion between us in relation to the construction of the provision of the Constitution which affects the question at issue. We all agree that until the consent of Congress is given, there can be no valid compact or agreement between States. And that, although the point of time when Congress may give its consent is not material, yet, when it is given, there must be a reciprocal and concurrent consent of the three parties to the contract. Without this, it is not a completed compact. If, therefore, Virginia withdrew its assent before the consent of Congress was given, there was no compact within the meaning of the Constitution." *Ibid.,*

pp. 63-64. These Justices considered the agreement as to erection of the new State inapplicable to the contested counties, "For though the second section of the first article of the new constitution had proposed to include it, the proposal was accompanied with conditions which were not complied with; and when that constitution was presented to Congress for approval, the proposal had already been rejected, and had no significance or effect whatever." *Ibid.*, p. 65.

[19] *Cf. The Constitution of the United States of America: Annotations of Cases Decided by the Supreme Court of the United States to January 1, 1938,* Senate Document No. 232, 74th Congress, 2d session (Washington, D.C.: U.S. Government Printing Office, 1938), p. 370.

[20] 148 U.S. 503 (1893). See *supra,* Ch. II, for treatment of other aspects of this case.

[21] *Ibid.*, p. 521. [22] *Ibid.*

[23] *Ibid.*, p. 522. *Cf. Green* v. *Biddle,* 8 Wheat. (21 U.S.) 1, 85-87 (1823), and *Wharton* v. *Wise,* 153 U.S. 15, 173 (1894). In the latter it is stated: "The consent of Congress to any agreement or compact between two or more States is sufficiently indicated, when not necessary to be made in advance, by the adoption or approval of proceedings taken under it." See *supra,* Ch. II, for treatment of cases.

[24] *Virginia* v. *Tennessee,* 148 U.S. 503, 522 (1893). *Cf. Russell* v. *American Association,* 139 Tenn. 124, 201 S.W. 151 (1918), and *North Carolina* v. *Tennessee,* 235 U.S. 1 (1914), in connection with the doctrine of implied consent.

[25] *Virginia* v. *Tennessee,* 148 U.S. 503, 518 (1893). See Chapter II for list of hypothetical compacts or agreements for which it would not be necessary to obtain the consent of Congress.

[26] Carman, *op. cit.*, p. 282.

[27] "Regional Education: A New Use of the Interstate Compact?" *Virginia Law Review,* 34:66, January, 1948. This article is initialed W.P.M. See also "Legal Problems Relating to Interstate Compacts." *Iowa Law Review,* 23:624, May, 1938, and "Some Legal and Practical Problems of the Interstate Compact." *Yale Law Journal,* 45:327, December, 1935. In the latter it is stated: ". . . such a result is unwarranted, for the Constitution requires Congressional consent to any interstate compact or agreement. If the arrangement is . . . a compact . . . , consent should be required without reference to its subject matter."

[28] See *supra,* Ch. II. A new turn may be presaged by dicta of the Court in *West Virginia ex rel Dyer* v. *Sims,* 341 U.S. 22, 27 (1951), wherein it was said with respect to the Ohio River Valley Water Sanitation Compact that congressional consent was required "as for all compacts." See *supra,* Ch. II, for treatment of this case in connection with the matter of Supreme Court "Jurisdiction" and *infra,* Ch. V, for a treatment of the compact involved as one of the uses to which the compact device has been put.

[29] Charles E. Hughes, *Addresses and Papers of Charles Evans Hughes* (New York and London: G. P. Putnam's Sons, 1908), p. 139. Perhaps it is unfair to take the words of Chief Justice Hughes literally. Professor Hart points out that "What the court *says* . . . is not the law of the land. . . . *Dicta* — things said — are not binding under *stare decisis. Stare decisis* does not mean *stare dictis.*" James Hart, *An Introduction to Administrative Law, with Selected Cases* (2nd edition; New York: Appleton-Century-Crofts, Inc., 1950), p. 20.

[30] *McHenry County* v. *Brady,* 163 N.W. 540, 37 N.D. 59 (1917). See *supra,* Ch. II, for details and general treatment of this case. The highest court of North

Dakota pointed out that, although there was language in the case of *Holmes* v. *Jennison* which seemed to preclude any intercourse between a State and a foreign state, the later decisions of the Court "seem to adopt the theory that not all intercourse is forbidden, or contracts prohibited, but only those agreements or compacts which affect the supremacy of the United States, or its political rights, or which tend in any measure to increase the political power of the states as against the United States or between themselves." *Ibid.*, p. 544.

[31] *Dover* v. *Portsmouth Bridge*, 17 N.H. 200 (1845).

[32] *Union Branch Rail Road Co.* v. *East Tennessee and Georgia R. R. Co.*, 14 Ga. 327 (1853). *Cf. Mackay* v. *New York, N. H. & H. R. Co.*, 82 Conn. 73, 72 Atl. 583 (1909), following *St. Louis & San Francisco Railway* v. *James*, 161 U.S. 545 (1896), in which Mr. Justice Shiras said for the Court that "It is competent for a railroad corporation organized under the laws of one State, when authorized so to do by the consent of the State which created it, to accept authority from another State to extend its railroad into such State and to receive a grant of powers to own and control, by lease or purchase, railroads therein, and to subject itself to such rules and regulations as may be prescribed by the second State. Such legislation on the part of two or more States is not, in the absence of inhibitory legislation by Congress, regarded as within the constitutional prohibition of agreements or compacts between States." p. 562.

[33] *Fisher* v. *Steele*, 39 La. Ann. 447, 1 South. 882 (1887). See *supra*, Ch. II, for treatment of this case. See also *Dixie Wholesale Grocery* v. *Martin*, 278 Ky. 705, 129 S.W. (2d) 181 (1939), and C. Ben Dutton, "Compacts and Trade Barrier Controversies," *Indiana Law Journal*, 16:208, December, 1940.

[34] *James* v. *Dravo Contracting Co.*, 302 U.S. 134, 148 (1937). *Arizona* v. *California*, 292 U.S. 341, 345 (1934) was cited as authority.

[35] *James* v. *Dravo Contracting Co.*, 302 U.S. 134, 148 (1937).

[36] 45 United States *Statutes at Large* 1057, Ch. 42.

[37] See *supra*, Ch. I, for treatment of general aspects of prior congressional consent and subsequent congressional approval.

[38] See *supra*, Ch. I.

[39] "Legal Problems Relating to Interstate Compacts." *Iowa Law Review*, 23:624, May, 1938.

CHAPTER IV

A CRUCIAL AREA: ENFORCEMENT

Failure on the part of one State to fulfill the terms of a compact with another could be expected to lead to a suit within the original jurisdiction of the Supreme Court to secure the performance of the compact. The question of enforcement of an interstate compact is equivalent in the final analysis to the question of the power of the Supreme Court to enforce a judgment rendered by it against a State of the Union.[1] The extended controversy between Virginia and West Virginia over settlement of the debt question led the Court to consider its powers to compel obedience and to clarify somewhat the course of action which it would pursue in the face of threatened disobedience.

In the case of *Green* v. *Biddle*, it may be recalled, the Court indicated that "the duty not less than the power of this court . . . to declare a law unconstitutional, which impairs the obligation of contracts, whoever may be the parties to them, is too clearly enjoyed [enjoined?] by the constitution itself, and too firmly established by the decisions of this and other courts, to be now shaken . . ."[2] A State is prohibited by the contract impairment clause of the Constitution from impairing its compacts with other States. Professor W. W. Willoughby points out "that, in appropriate cases, the court has issued injunctions to State officials, and, in boundary disputes has awarded to individual States jurisdiction over areas claimed by other States. Disregard of these injunctions would undoubtedly have been followed by proceedings in contempt, and the executive branch of the Federal Government would presumably have given armed assistance, if required, in order to enable the States to which disputed territory was awarded to exercise political jurisdiction over such territory, had the States adversely affected attempted to continue to exercise authority thereover."[3]

Money judgments against a State were sought or entered on various occasions prior to the Court's consideration of the Virginia-West Virginia controversy. In *United States* v. *North Carolina*[4] the Court in the exercise of original and uncontested jurisdiction entertained an action of debt brought by the United States against North Carolina upon bonds issued by the State and held by the United States. North Carolina some time after the maturity of the bonds paid the principal, together with interest thereon to the time when the bonds became payable. According to the Court the only question presented for its decision was whether, as matter of law, the bonds bore interest after maturity. The legal principle prevalent in North Carolina under decisions of the Supreme Court of North Carolina was that the State, unless by or pursuant to an explicit statute, was not liable for interest even on a definite sum which was overdue and unpaid. Applying that principle the Court held that the State was not liable for interest. Thus no question of enforcement arose in the case.

In *United States* v. *Michigan*[5] the Court entertained an original bill in equity against the State of Michigan for an accounting and, overruling the Michigan demurrer, granted leave to answer. In case Michigan refuses to plead further, the Court held, "the judgment will be in favor of the United States for an accounting and for the payment of the sum found due thereon."[6] Subsequent dismissal of the case on motion of the United States, however, precluded any question of enforcement of the Court's judgment.[7]

In the case of *South Dakota* v. *North Carolina*[8] the Court rendered a money judgment which the defendant State subsequently paid. South Dakota brought an original suit in the Supreme Court to compel North Carolina to pay some North Carolina bonds which South Dakota possessed. The bonds were secured by a mortgage of railroad stock owned by North Carolina. The North Carolina counsel touched the crux of the problem underlying enforcement of a Supreme Court money judgment against a State when they stated that "A suit cannot usually be maintained against a State to compel the payment of its debts, as it might necessitate an interference with, if not the complete control and direction of, the legislative function of assessing, levying, collecting and distributing taxes, which is, as yet, beyond the competency of courts; there is no means of rendering the decree effective, unless this court is prepared to appoint a receiver with the extraordinary powers of taking charge of and administering the affairs of a delinquent State."[9] In respect to this statement the Court observed that it was confronted with the contention that it lacked the power to enforce such a judgment, and that such lack of power was conclusive evidence that, notwithstanding the general language of the Constitution, there was an implied exception of actions brought to recover money from a State. Citing *Meriwether* v. *Garrett*,[10] the Court pointed out that the public property held by a State or local government agency is exempt from seizure upon execution because it is held, not as a part of its private assets, but as a trust for public purposes. And as a rule a municipality does not hold private property subject to be taken upon execution. Moreover, the Court admitted that a levy of taxes is not within the scope of the judicial power except as it commands an inferior municipality to execute the power granted by the legislature. In support of the point the Court quoted its earlier opinion in *Rees* v. *City of Watertown:*

"We are of the opinion that this court has not the power to direct a tax to be levied for the payment of these judgments. This power to impose burdens and raise money is the highest attribute of sovereignty, and is exercised, first, to raise money for public purposes only; and, second, by the power of legislative authority only. It is a power that has not been extended to the judiciary. Especially is it beyond the power of the Federal judiciary to assume the place of a State in the exercise of this authority at once so delicate and so important." [11]

On the one hand there were the general language of the Constitution vesting jurisdiction in the Court over "controversies between two or more States," the cases of *Chisholm* v. *Georgia,*[12] *United States* v. *North Carolina,*[13] *and United States* v. *Michigan* [14] (in which the Court sustained jurisdiction over actions to recover money from a State), the manifest trend of other decisions, the necessity of some way of ending controversies between States, and the fact that this claim for the payment of money was one justiciable in its nature. On the other hand, there were certain individual opinions of justices of the Court, the difficulty of enforcing a judgment for money against a State by reason of its ordinary lack of private property subject to seizure upon execution, and the absolute inability of a court to compel a levy of taxes by the legislature. "Notwithstanding the embarrassments which suround the question," the Court stated, "it is directly presented and may have to be determined before the case is finally concluded, but for the present it is sufficient to state the question with its difficulties." [15]

The foregoing statement of the Court indicates its awareness of the fact that it was presented with the question of the Court's power to enforce a money judgment. In *South Dakota* v. *North Carolina,* however, the bonds were secured by a mortgage of railroad stock owned by the State, and this fact greatly simplified the problem of the Court. A decree was entered which, after finding the amount due on the bonds and that the bonds were secured by one hundred shares of the stock of the North Carolina Railroad Company belonging to North Carolina, ordered North Carolina to pay the amount due together with costs of the suit to South Dakota on or before January 1, 1905. The decree further ordered that in default of such payment an order of sale be issued, directing the Marshal of the Court to sell at public auction the interest of the State of North Carolina in the North Carolina Railroad Company to satisfy the judgment.

North Carolina paid the amount which the Court decreed due

South Dakota. "But," as Mr. William C. Coleman asks, "suppose it is otherwise? Suppose the defendant State refuses to pay, pursuant to a decree entered by the Supreme Court against it in favor of another State, will the Court *actually compel* payment?"[16] The *North Carolina* case gave every indication that payment would actually be compelled where the State holds private property which can be sold to satisfy the judgment.

In the extended controversy between Virginia and West Virginia over settlement of the debt issue the question of the Court's power of enforcement of a money decree was reconsidered, and the Court at least took a positive stand on the question — a stand which was forced by West Virginia's non-compliance with the terms of the Court's decree, and that stand was a flat assertion of the Court's power to enforce its decree.

It has been remarked that "Virginia and West Virginia are the most litigious States of the American Union, if tested by the frequency with which they have resorted to the Supreme Court, Virginia having been twelve times a plaintiff and twice a defendant in suits between the States. And West Virginia, although a newcomer in the Union of States, has been a party to twelve suits, each time a defendant, and of these twelve no less than ten were with the State of Virginia, all arising out of the separation of the Western counties of the State during the Civil War and their formation into a State of the Union."[17] The first of these cases[18] was that, already considered above, in which the right of the State of West Virginia to the counties of Berkeley and Jefferson was confirmed by the Court. The second[19] began a series of nine concerned with the financial, as contrasted with the territorial, situation created by the partition of Virginia and formation of the new State of West Virginia. As James Brown Scott states, "The question, although varying in each, is one and the same: the amount of indebtedness of the State of Virginia incurred before the separation which in law and in equity should be assumed and paid by the State of West Virginia."[20] Professor W. W. Willoughby indicates the underlying significance of the series in his observation that "In the suit of Virginia against West Virginia, which, in one form or another, was repeatedly before the Supreme Court, the issue finally narrowed itself down to whether the court was competent to order State officials, as such, to perform acts which their States had not directed them to perform."[21]

In the first of the series Chief Justice Fuller, who delivered the unanimous opinion of the Court assuming jurisdiction of the case, presented its historical background. The State of West Virginia was admitted into the Union June 20, 1863, upon the terms prescribed by

Virginia in ordinances adopted in convention and in acts passed by the General Assembly of the "Restored Government of the Commonwealth," giving her consent to the formation of a new State out of her territory. The people of the "would-be State," assembled in convention, adopted an ordinance to provide for the formation of the new State. The ninth section of that ordinance provided that "The new State shall take upon itself a just proportion of the public debt of the Commonwealth of Virginia, prior to the first day of January, 1861, to be ascertained by charging to it all state expenditures within the limits thereof, and a just proportion of the ordinary expenses of the state government, since any part of said debt was contracted; and deducting therefrom the monies paid into the treasury of the Commonwealth from the counties included within the said new State during the same period." [22] Virginia's consent to the formation of the new State was predicated upon this condition. On February 3 and 4, 1863, the General Assembly of the "Restored State of Virginia" enacted two statutes in pursuance of which money and property amounting to and of the value of several millions of dollars were transferred to West Virginia.

Article VIII of the constitution under which West Virginia was admitted to the Union provided in part that "No debt shall be contracted by this State, except . . . to redeem a previous liability of the State. . . ," [23] that "The legislature may at any time direct a sale of the stocks owned by the State in banks and other corporations, but [that] the proceeds of such sale shall be applied to the liquidation of the public debt. . . ," [24] and that an "equitable proportion" of the public debt of Virginia, prior to January 1, 1861, "shall be assumed by this State; and the legislature shall ascertain the same as soon as may be practicable, and provide for the liquidation thereof, by a sinking fund sufficient to pay the accruing interest, and redeem the principal within thirty-four years." [25] These provisions were construed to indicate that the "public debt" and the "previous liability" manifestly referred to a portion of the public debt of the original State of Virginia and liability for the money and property of the original State which had been received by West Virginia, while the provisions for the assumption and liquidation of the equitable portion of Virginia's public debt were obviously framed in compliance with the conditions on which the consent of Virginia was given to the creation of the State of West Virginia and the money and property were transferred.

From 1865 to 1905 various efforts were made by Virginia through its constituted authorities to effect an adjustment and settlement with West Virginia of an equitable proportion of the public debt of the undivided State proper to be borne and paid by West Virginia. All these efforts proved unavailing, because West Virginia refused or failed to take any action or do anything to bring about a settlement or an adjustment with Virginia. Virginia invoked the original jurisdiction of the Court to procure a decree for an accounting as between the two States.

West Virginia demurred to the Virginia bill, asserting that the Court lacked jurisdiction because the matters set forth in the bill did not constitute such a controversy or such controversies as could be heard and determined by the Court, and because the Court lacked power to enforce and therefore power to render any final judgment or decree therein. [26] The Court rejected West Virginia's contention, pointing out that the object of the suit was a settlement with West Virginia, and to that end a determination and adjudication of the amount due by that State to Virginia, and that it was not to be presumed on demurrer that West Virginia would refuse to carry out the decree of the Court when the Court had adjudged the proportion of the debt of the original State which it would be equitable for West Virginia to pay. West Virginia consented to be sued when she was admitted into the Union, and it must be assumed that the legislature of West Virginia would in the natural course make provision for the satisfaction of any decree which might be rendered. Absolute assertion of repudiation of the decree would present the proper time for consideration of means for its enforcement.

West Virginia advanced another reason for the lack of jurisdiction in the Court in the form of an alleged compact entered into between Virginia and West Virginia, with the consent of Congress, by which the question of the liability of West Virginia to Virginia was submitted to the arbitrament and award of the legislature of West Virginia as the sole tribunal which could pass upon it. When Virginia provided for the formation of a new State out of her territory and declared that "the new State shall take upon itself a just proportion of the public debt of the Commonwealth of Virginia prior to the first day of January, 1861," to be ascertained as provided, [27] it was to be supposed that the new State had this in mind when it framed its own constitution. When that constitution provided that its legislature should "ascertain the same as soon as practicable," presumably it referred to the method of ascertainment prescribed by the Virginia convention. What was meant by the expression that the "legislature shall ascertain the same" was that the legislature should ascertain as soon as practicable the result of the pursuit of the method prescribed and provide for the liquidation of the amount so ascertained. Chief Justice Fuller indicated the basic flaw inherent in West Virginia's argument by his observation that "it may well be inquired why, in the forty-three years that have elapsed since the alleged compact was entered into, West Virginia has never indicated that she stood upon such a compact, and, if so, why no step has ever been taken by West Virginia to enter upon the performance of the duty which such 'compact' imposed, and to notify Virginia that she was ready and willing to discharge such duty."[28] This and other questions, however, were not to be decided on demurrer. Hence the Court, having decided merely that it had jurisdiction, overruled West Virginia's demurrer, although without prejudice to any question, and gave West Virginia leave to answer the Virginia complaint by the first Monday of the next term.

West Virginia availed itself of the leave of the Court and filed its answer to the Virginia bill, argument being relative to the form of the decree referring the controversy to a master for investigation. In this, the second phase of the case, the decree of the Court indicated the principles which were to guide the master and required the cooperation of the States in litigation.[29]

The next and third phase of the dispute turned upon the report of the master. Mr. Justice Holmes, speaking for the Court, indicated that the case was to be considered in an untechnical spirit, as no municipal code governed the matter, and that the Court might be called on to adjust differences which could not be dealt with by Congress or disposed of by the legislature of either State alone. Holmes pointed out that it was held by the Court in 1870 that the provisions of the West Virginia constitution consented to by the Restored State of Virginia constituted an agreement between the old State and the new, and that so much might be taken practically to have been decided again upon the demurrer in the first phase of this case, although the demurrer was overruled without prejudice to any question. He proceeded to reassert this holding, observing that the consent of the legislature of the Restored State was a consent to the admission of West Virginia under the provisions set forth in the constitution for the would-be State, and that Congress gave its sanction only on the basis of that constitution and the consent of Virginia. "These three documents would establish a contract without more."[30] By the contract between Virginia and West Virginia, West Virginia must be taken to have promised to Virginia to pay her share, whoever might be the persons to whom payment ultimately was to be made. In answer to the West Virginia contention that the question of West Virginia's liability was submitted by the "agreement" to the arbitrament and award of the West Virginia legislature as the sole tribunal which could pass upon it, it was indicated that the provision in the constitution of the State of West Virginia that the legislature shall ascertain the proportion as soon as may be practicable was not intended to undo the contract by making the representative and mouthpiece of one of the parties the sole tribunal for its enforcement. It was simply an exhortation and command from supreme to subordinate authority to perform the promise as soon as might be and an indication of the way in which it should be performed. What is just and equitable is a judicial question similar to many that arise in private litigation and is within the competence of a tribunal to decide. Thus the contract was to be the measure of the liability of the State of West Virginia, and the Court was competent to determine what constituted West Virginia's "just and equitable proportion of the public debt." At this stage of the case a provisional estimate of West Virginia's share of the principal debt was made, although the question of interest was left for subsequent consideration. It was deemed best at this stage to go no farther, but to await the effect of a conference between the parties, which must be held whatever its outcome. If the cause were to be pressed contentiously to the end, however, it was to be referred to a master to go over the figures given provisionally, and to make such calculations as might become necessary. [31]

Virginia's attempts to arrange a conference met with little cooperation, and, after a period of a little more than seven months from the date of the Court's "recommendation" that the States confer, Virginia initiated the fourth phase of the controversy by moving that the Court proceed to determine all questions left open by its last decision. [32] West Virginia counsel opposed the Virginia motion on the ground that the only body in West Virginia competent to act upon the debt question was the state legislature, and the Court should not act on the question until the legislature could convene in regular session. Mr. Justice Holmes, again speaking for the Court, sanctioned West Virginia's inactivity, stating that "a State cannot be expected to move with the celerity of a private business man; it is enough if it proceeds, in the language of the English Chancery, with all deliberate speed." [33] James Brown Scott observes that "Language such as this clearly implies a belief on the part of the learned Justice and of the Court, whose unanimous opinion he delivered, that the objection was interposed for delay, as the co-operation of the Legislature did not seem necessary for a conference of this kind." [34] Yet the West Virginia view was accepted, the Court overruling the Virginia motion without prejudice.

Somewhat over two years later Virginia again brought a motion before the Court, which was virtually a reiteration of the former motion to proceed and was based upon the ground that certain negotiations which had taken place between the Virginia Debt Commission representing Virginia and a Commission representing West Virginia, appointed in virtue of a joint resolution of the legislature of that State adopted in 1913, made it certain that there was no hope of an adjustment.[35] West Virginia counsel insisted that the Virginia view of the negotiations was a misapprehension of West Virginia's purposes and requested a six-month reprieve to enable the West Virginia Commission "to complete its labors." The Court in this, the fifth phase of the dispute, granted West Virginia's request, although it reduced the time asked and directed that the case be assigned for final hearing on the 13th day of April, 1914, to prevent the possibility of the case running into the succeeding term.

At the time set by the Court for the "final hearing" West Virginia prayed leave to be permitted to file a supplemental answer asserting the existence of credits, which "if properly considered" would materially reduce the sum fixed as due to the State of Virginia, the answer in addition asserting various grounds why interest should not be allowed on the sum due.[36] Virginia counsel objected, stating that the items embraced in the supplemental answer had in effect already entered into the considerations by which the principal sum due was fixed, and that if not, the case should not be postponed for the purpose of permitting the rights urged in the answer to be availed of, because every item concerning such alleged rights was proved in the case before the master, was mentioned in his report, and was known or could have been known "by the use of ordinary diligence by those representing West Virginia."[37] The Court granted the West Virginia request, ordering that the subject matter of the supplemental answer be considered traversed by Virginia and be at once referred to the master for consideration and report and further directing that the proceedings before the master be so conducted as to secure a report on or before the second Monday of October, 1914.

In 1915 in the seventh phase of the case Mr. Justice Hughes, delivering the unanimous opinion of the Court, rendered a judgment against the State of West Virginia, decreeing that that State should pay to the State of Virginia $12,393,929.50 with interest. The judgment was based upon three propositions specifically found to be established: (1) that when territory was carved out of Virginia for the purpose of constituting the area of West Virginia, the new State at its inception became bound for and assumed the obligation to pay its just share of the previous public debt of Virginia; (2) that the West Virginia obligation was the subject of a contract between the two States, made with the consent of Congress and incorporated into the constitution by which West Virginia was admitted by Congress into the Union, and that the obligation became thereby a condition of admission and part of the "very governmental fiber" of that State; and (3) that the sum of the judgment rendered constituted the equitable share of the Virginia debt due by West Virginia in accordance with her contractual obligation.[38]

Presumably the Justices deemed this decree the end of the dispute. Yet, the dilatory tactics of West Virginia and that State's generally uncooperative attitude throughout the controversy may have given the Court forewarning of the State's subsequent failure to comply with the ruling. Be that as it may, issuance of the decree did not end the controversy. One salient difference distinguishes this decree from that rendered in *South Dakota* v. *North Carolina* treated above: no specific property or state revenue was pledged for the payment of the West Virginia obligation. Thus attachment and sale under a writ of execution of such property was not possible in this case as it was in the earlier one.

A year after the decree of the Court was rendered, Virginia petitioned the Court for a writ of execution against West Virginia on the ground that the latter State had taken no steps whatever to provide for the payment of the decree. West Virginia opposed the granting of the execution on three grounds: (1) because her legislature, which alone possessed the power to take the action necessary for payment of the judgment in question, had not met since rendition of the judgment, and issuance of an execution before its next meeting would deprive West Virginia of the opportunity to accept and abide by the Court's decision and to make provision for its satisfaction without compulsion; (2) because presumptively West Virginia possessed no property subject to execution; and (3) because, although the Supreme Court is granted by the Constitution jurisdiction over controversies between States and therefore authority to render the decree in question, no authority was conferred to enforce a money judgment against a State if such a judgment were rendered in the exercise of that jurisdiction.[39] The Court deemed the first ground adequate reason for not granting the motion at that time. Hence Virginia's prayer for the issuance of a writ of execution was denied but without prejudice to its renewal after the next session of the legislature of the State of West Virginia had met and had a reasonable opportunity to provide for payment of the judgment.

The West Virginia legislature met and failed to take action directed to compliance with the Court's decree. On January 29, 1917, Virginia instituted the ninth phase of the Virginia-West Virginia controversy by submitting her motion for leave to file a petition for a writ of mandamus, and for an order directed to the State of West Virginia and the members of her legislature requiring them to show cause why the writ should not issue commanding the levy of a tax to satisfy the judgment rendered by the Court. The motion was granted on February 5,

1917, and the rule issued returnable on March 6th.[40] West Virginia interposed a motion to discharge the rule requiring her to show cause, and the instant decision resulted from the case upon the rule to show cause and the motion to dismiss the case.

Chief Justice White delivered the opinion of the Court, asserting, as Mr. Willoughby words it, the Court's "right to enforce its judgment by appropriate remedies, even though the application of such remedies might operate upon the governmental powers of the State."[41] In all the cases decided between States as such, the States against which judgments were given voluntarily complied with those judgments. But in *South Dakota* v. *North Carolina*[42] it was remarked that doubt had been expressed in some instances by individual judges as to whether the original jurisdiction conferred on the Court by the Constitution embraced the right of one State to recover a judgment in a mere action for debt against another. The Court did not solve the suggested doubt, however, for the question was not before it. Moreover, the question thus left open had no bearing upon and did not require consideration in the instant case; first, because the power to render the judgment as between the two States, enforcement of which was under consideration, was foreclosed as to them by the fact of its rendition, and second, because, while the controversy between the States culminated in a decree for money and that subject was within the issues, nevertheless, the generating cause of the controversy was the carving out of the dominion of one of the States the area composing the other and the resulting expressly assumed obligation of the newly created State to pay the just proportion of the preexisting debt, an obligation which rested in contract between the two States, consented to by Congress and expressed in substance as a condition in the Constitution by which the new State was admitted into the Union.[43]

Both parties admitted that West Virginia owned no property not used for governmental purposes and that, therefore, on the mere issue of an execution, the judgment was not susceptible of being enforced if, under such an execution, property actually devoted to immediate governmental uses of the State might not be taken. The contentions on either side were disposed of by considering two subjects: first, the limitations on the right to enforce inhering in the fact that the judgment was against a State and its enforcement against a State as a governmental being; and second, the appropriateness of the form of procedure for such an enforcement. These subjects were considered in the form of two questions: "1. *May a judgment rendered against a State . . . be enforced against it as such, including the right, to the extent necessary for so doing, of exerting authority over the governmental powers and agen-*

cies possessed by the State?" [44] "2. *What are the appropriate remedies for such enforcement?"* [45]

Virginia contended that the Contitution subjected West Virginia to judicial authority at the suit of Virginia, and, therefore, the judgment rendered in such a suit binds and operates upon the State of West Virginia in its governmental capacity, including all instrumentalities and agencies of state power, and indirectly binding the whole body of citizens of that State and the property which, by the exertion of powers possessed by the State, are subject to taxation for the purpose of meeting and discharging the state obligation. The inability to enforce by means of ordinary process of execution, then, gives the right and sanctions the exertion of the authority to enforce the judgment by compelling the legislature to exercise its power of taxation. Virginia buttressed her contention with references to many cases in which it was held that, where a municipality is authorized to levy specified taxation to pay particular indebtedness, the judicial power may enforce the levy of the tax to meet a judgment rendered as a consequence of default in paying that indebtedness. [46]

West Virginia counsel countered with the contention that West Virginia as a State may not, as to powers of government reserved to it by the Constitution, be controlled or limited by process for the purpose of enforcing the payment of the judgment. Counsel distinguishd between property owned by the State and not used for a governmental purpose and state property used for a governmental purpose, denying that execution could properly be issued against the latter. The distinction was deemed by West Virginia counsel to render the cases relied upon by Virginia inapplicable to the right of coercing the State to exercise its power of taxation to create a fund from which the judgment could be paid. West Virginia counsel insisted that the rights reserved to the States by the Constitution may not be interfered with by the judicial power merely because the judicial power has been given authority to adjudicate at the instance of one State a right asserted against another State, since, although the authority to enforce the adjudication may not be denied, execution to give effect to that authority is restrained by the provisions of the Constitution which recognize state governmental power. The West Virginia contentions were rejected as incompatible with and destructive of numerous cases decided by the Court.

When the Constitution gave original jurisdiction to the Supreme Court to entertain at the instance of one State a suit against another, the intention must have been to modify the general rule of immunity of sovereign States from judicial power, that is, to bring the States and their governmental authority within the exceptional judicial power which was created. No other rational explanation can be given for the provision. This conception of the operation and effect of the right to exert, at the prayer of one State, judicial authority over another is given force by the context of the Constitution, the express prohibition which it contains as to the power of the States to contract with each other except with the consent of Congress, and the limitations as to war and armies, obviously intended to prevent resort to force by the States for the redress of any grievance. It was not a want of authority in Congress to decide controversies between States under the Articles of Confederation, but the absence of power in Congress to enforce its decisions on such subjects as against the governments of the States which was the evil that cried aloud for cure. It is patent that the provisions written into the Constitution—the power which was conferred upon Congress and the judicial power as to the States, joined with the prohibitions placed upon the States—all combined to unite the authority to decide with the power to enforce, "a unison which could only have arisen from contemplating the dangers of the past and the unalterable purpose to prevent their recurrence in the future."[47] As a general proposition, moreover, it is elementary that judicial power essentially involves the right to enforce the results of its exertion.[48]

It was, therefore, held with respect to whether a judgment rendered against a State as a State may be enforced against it as such to the extent of exercising authority over the governmental powers possessed by the State, that the State "as a governmental entity" was subjected by the Constitution to the judicial power under the conditions stated, and that the duty to enforce the judgment by resort to appropriate remedies was certain, "even although their exertion may operate upon the governmental powers of the State."[49]

Appropriate remedies for such enforcement were then considered. This section of the opinion was opened with the statement that "the powers to render the judgment and to enforce it arise from the grant in the Constitution on that subject, looked at from a generic point of view," that "both are federal powers," and that, "comprehensively considered," they are "sustained by every authority of the federal government, judicial, legislative or executive, which may be appropriately exercised."[50] The treatment of this section, confined to a determination of the remedies appropriate in view of the particular judgment in the instant cause, was broken down into two parts treating the subjects of (a) the power of Congress to legislate to secure the enforcement of the contract between the States, and (b) the appropriate remedies which might be exerted by the judicial power to enforce the judgment. With respect to the first of these it was observed that vesting in Congress complete power to control agreements between States virtually endowed Congress with the ultimate power of decision as to whether an agreement might or might not be made, which was withdrawing that decision from state authority and bringing it within the federal power.

The power of Congress to legislate for the enforcement of the West Virginia obligation is "two-fold," *i.e.*, it can legislate to secure enforcement, or it can legislate to add to the power of the judiciary remedies to meet the exigency. Beyond the possibility that Congress might add to the existent judicial remedies, no indication was given as to any specific legislative course which Congress might pursue to secure enforcement. The second legislative course indicated would seem to be included in the first as merely a particular exercise of the general power to legislate to secure enforcement. The power of Congress to disapprove or to assent to a contract between States by necessary implication carried with it the right, if the contract were assented to and hence became operative by the will of Congress, to see to its enforcement.

Since Congress was endowed with the power to provide for the execution of the contract, that power must be plenary and complete, limited only by the general rule that the acts done for its exertion must be relevant and appropriate to the power. It follows that, by the very fact that the national power is paramount in the area over which it extends, "the lawful exertion of its authority by Congress to compel compliance with the obligation resulting from the contract between the two States which it approved is not circumscribed by the powers reserved to the States."[51] Moreover, "the power of Congress to exert its legislative authority . . . also extends to the creation of new remedies in addition to those provided for by § 14 of the Judiciary Act of 1789 . . . to meet the exigency occasioned by the judicial duty of enforcing a judgment against a State under the circumstances as here disclosed."[52] Thus if the power of the Court is insufficient, Congress may overcome that insufficiency. And Congress is the proper body to overcome it, for provision by legislative action of additional process relevant to the enforcement of judicial authority is the exertion of a legislative and not the exercise of a judicial power.

In consideration of the appropriate remedies which might be exerted by the judicial power to enforce the judgment, it was observed that insofar as the duty to award a mandamus commanding the levy by the West Virginia legislature of a tax to pay the judgment was disputed merely because authority to enforce a judgment against a State may not affect state power, the contention was already adversely disposed of.

Yet this did not dispose of all the contentions between the parties on the subject, since, on the one hand, it was insisted that the existence of a discretion in the legislature of West Virginia as to taxation precluded the possibility of issuing the order, and on the other hand, it was contended that the duty to give effect to the judgment against the State, operating upon all state powers, excluded the legislative discretion asserted and gave the resulting right to compel. The Court apparently was loath to exercise the right to enforce its judgment against a State *qua* State, which it had asserted, and chose not to dispose at that time of the issue posed by the conflicting Virginia and West Virginia contentions. Nor did the Court determine the question, which it had been led to consider on its own motion, whether there is power to direct the levy of a tax adequate to pay the judgment and provide for its enforcement "irrespective of state agencies."[53] The forbearance of the Court was based on the hope that, if it refrained at this time from passing upon these questions, it might "be spared in the future the necessity of exerting compulsory power against one of the States of the Union to compel it to discharge a plain duty resting upon it under the Constitution."[54] The Court was of the opinion that it should not finally dispose of the case but, because of the character of the parties and the nature of the controversy—a contract approved by Congress and subject to be enforced by it—should reserve further action in order that full opportunity might be afforded to Congress "to exercise the power which it undoubtedly possesses."[55]

The conclusions of the Court were that the judgment against the State, operating upon it in all its governmental powers, and the duty to enforce it viewed in that aspect were matters "irrevocably foreclosed" and that the case should be restored to the docket for argument of the three questions left open: 1. The right under the conditions previously stated to award the mandamus prayed for; 2. If not, the power and duty to direct the levy of a tax as stated; and 3. If means for doing so be found to exist, the right, if necessary, to apply such other and appropriate equitable remedy, by dealing with the funds or taxable property of West Virginia or the rights of that State, as may secure an execution of the judgment.

These questions were never answered by the Court, for Virginia entered acknowledgment of satisfaction of the decree on March 1, 1920. West Virginia apparently believed the old maxim: "Where there is a will, there is a way." Certainly the Court had flatly asserted its power to enforce its decree.

Although the questions reserved by the Court for future decision remain unanswered certain elements relative to the general question of enforcement of a judgment rendered against a State are disposed of by the Court's holding. The Court has concluded that the right to enforce its judgment is inherent in the judicial power and that that right is operative against a State which has consented in adoption of the Constitution to suit by another State. Moreover, the judgment may be enforced against the State, *qua* State, operative upon its governmental agencies and property used for governmental purposes, as well as property held by the State in a proprietary capacity. Congress possesses the power to adopt such measures as are necessary to force the State's compliance with the judgment of the Court rendered in the constitutional exercise of the judicial power and also the power to add to existing judicial remedies to enable the Court to meet the problem precipitated by the judicial duty of enforcing its judgment against a State in such circumstance. And with respect to interstate compacts for the validity of which congressional consent is necessary, the Court has indicated that implicit in the power to assent is the power to see to the compact's enforcement, once it has been "assented to" and hence become "operative by the will of Congress." All in all, it might be said that the Court's decision in *Virginia* v. *West Virginia* renders the obligation of the compact, which the Court once said "is 'the law which binds the parties to perform their agreement'," [56] virtually certain. Thus it would seem that the Council of State Governments is quite right in answering those who contend that compacts are too flexible and cannot be enforced with the observation that:

"As far as a mutual exchange of state resources or state privileges is concerned, this criticism seems unfounded. The Supreme Court in *Virginia* v. *West Virginia* (1918) indicated that it would find means of enforcing an accounting of interstate indebtedness. Enforcement of other . . . compacts must be left to the courts. The precedent, established a century and a half ago, that no American state will refuse to obey the decision of the Supreme Court in an interstate suit, makes it seem likely that most compacts can be readily enforced." [57]

The opposite criticism that compacts constitute an inflexible mode of "legislation" and lead to irrevocable results may be less susceptible to dispute.

[1] For treatments of the leading case and in general of the power of the Supreme Court to enforce a judgment rendered by it against a State, see: Thomas Reed Powell, "Coercing a State to Pay a Judgment: Virginia v. West Virginia." *Michigan Law Review*, 17:1, November, 1918; Westel W. Willoughby, *The Constitutional Law of the United States* (2d edition; New York: Baker, Voorhis and Company, 1929), III, Ch. LXXIX; William C. Coleman, "The State as Defendant under the Federal Constitution: The Virginia-West Virginia Debt Controversy." *Harvard Law Review*, 31:210, December, 1917; Joseph R. Long, "The Enforce-

ment of Judgments against a State." *Virginia Law Review,* 4:157, December, 1916; James B. Scott, *Judicial Settlement of Controversies between States of the American Union; An Analysis of Cases Decided in the Supreme Court of the United States* (Oxford: At the Clarendon Press, 1919), Ch. X.

[2] 8 Wheat. (21 U.S.) 1, 91-92 (1823). See *supra,* Ch. II, for treatment of *Green* v. *Biddle.*

[3] Willoughby, *op. cit.,* III, 1436. Failure to secure enforcement of a decree because of the lack of provision by the President of executive aid for its enforcement, as was the case in *Worcester* v. *Georgia,* 6 Pet. (31 U.S.) 515 (1832), does not touch the competence of the Court to give judgment, albeit it does render necessary the qualifying "presumably" in Professor Willoughby's statement.

[4] 136 U.S. 211 (1890). [5] 190 U.S. 379 (1903). [6] *Ibid.,* p. 406.

[7] 203 U.S. 601 (1906). [8] 192 U.S. 286 (1904). [9] *Ibid.,* pp. 300-301.

[10] 12 Otto (102 U.S.) 472, 513 (1880).

[11] 19 Wall. (86 U.S.) 107, 116-17 (1873). Attention was also drawn to *Heine* v. *The Levee Commissioners,* 19 Wall. (86 U.S.) 655, 661 (1873), and *Meriwether* v. *Garrett,* 12 Otto (102 U.S.) 472, 513 (1880).

[12] 2 Dall. 419 (1793). [13] See *supra,* Ch. IV, pp. 79-80.

[14] See *supra,* Ch. IV, p. 80.

[15] *South Dakota* v. *North Carolina,* 192 U.S. 286, 320-21 (1904).

[16] Coleman, *op. cit.,* p. 236.

[17] Scott, *Judicial Settlement of Controversies between States of the American Union; An Analysis of Cases Decided in the Supreme Court of the United States,* p. 453.

[18] *Virginia* v. *West Virginia,* 11 Wall. (78 U.S.) 39 (1870).

[19] *Virginia* v. *West Virginia,* 206 U.S. 290 (1907).

[20] Scott, *Judicial Settlement of Controversies between States of the American Union; An Analysis of Cases Decided in the Supreme Court of the United States,* p. 454.

[21] Willoughby, *op. Cit.,* III, 1437.

[22] *Virginia* v. *West Virginia,* 206 U.S. 290, 315-16 (1907).

[23] Section 5. [24] Section 7.

[25] Section 8; *Virginia* v. *West Virginia,* 206 U.S. 290, 316-17 (1907).

[26] The Chief Justice said that "We think these objections are disposed of by many decisions of this court." *Ibid.,* p. 317. Cited were *Cohens* v. *Virginia,* 6 Wheat. (19 U.S.) 264, 378, 406 (1821); *Kansas* v. *Colorado,* 185 U.S. 125 (1902); *Kansas* v. *Colorado,* 206 U.S. 46 (1907); *Missouri* v. *Illinois,* 180 U.S. 208 (1901); *Missouri* v. *Illinois,* 200 U.S. 496 (1906); *Georgia* v. *Tennessee Copper Company,* 206 U.S. 230 (1907); *United States* v. *Texas,* 143 U.S. 621 (1892); *United States* v. *North Carolina,* 136 U.S. 211 (1890); *United States* v. *Michigan,* 190 U.S. 379 (1903). By these cases, the Chief Justice stated, "and there are many more, it is established that, in the exercise of original jurisdiction as between States, this court necessarily in such a case as this has jurisdiction." *Virginia* v. *West Virginia,* 206 U.S. 290, 319 (1907).

[27] See *supra,* Ch. IV, p. 83, for provision as to ascertainment.

[28] *Virginia* v. *West Virginia,* 206 U.S. 290, 321 (1907).

[29] *Virginia* v. *West Virginia,* 209 U.S. 514 (1908).

[30] *Virginia* v. *West Virginia,* 220 U.S. 1, 28 (1911).

[31] *Ibid.,* p. 36. [32] *Virginia* v. *West Virginia,* 222 U.S. 17, 18 (1911).

[33] *Ibid.,* pp. 19-20.

[34] Scott, *Judicial Settlement of Controversies between States of the American*

Union; An Analysis of Cases Decided in the Supreme Court of the United States, p. 494.

[35] *Virginia* v. *West Virginia,* 231 U.S. 89, 90 (1913).

[36] *Virginia* v. *West Virginia,* 234 U.S. 117, 120 (1914). [37] *Ibid.*

[38] *Virginia* v. *West Virginia,* 238 U.S. 202 (1915).

[39] *Virginia* v. *West Virginia,* 241 U.S. 531, 532 (1916).

[40] *Virginia* v. *West Virginia,* 246 U.S. 565, 567 (1918).

[41] Willoughby, *op. cit.*, III, 1440. [42] 192 U.S. 286 (1904); *supra,* ch. IV.

[43] *Virginia* v. *West Virginia,* 246 U.S. 565, 592-93 (1918). Scott observes: "It is no doubt true that the present case is different from all of its predecessors, and it is difficult not to allow one's feelings to be coloured by the settled belief that West Virginia should satisfy the judgement of the Supreme Court in favour of Virginia, for the reason, if for none other, that its territory was severed from Virginia during the throes of a Civil War, in which that State could not defend itself or have its voice heard; that the party leaders in West Virginia responsible for the separation of the States felt impelled to assume at least a portion of the debt incurred by Virginia as far as it was expended in West Virginia; that the assumption of this equitable proportion of indebtedness was included in the State Constitution approved by the Congress, and to that extent is a contract, a constitutional provision of the State of West Virginia, and an act of Congress at one and the same time." Scott, *Judicial Settlement of Controversies between States of the American Union; An Analysis of Cases Decided in the Supreme Court of the United States,* p. 531.

[44] *Virginia* v. *West Virginia,* 246 U.S. 565, 593-94 (1918). [45] *Ibid.*, p. 600.

[46] Cases cited were *Supervisors* v. *United States,* 4 Wall. (71 U.S.) 435 (1866); *Von Hoffman* v. *City of Quincy,* 4 Wall. (71 U.S.) 535 (1866); *City of Galena* v. *Amy,* 5 Wall. (72 U.S.) 705 (1866); *Riggs* v. *Johnson County,* 6 Wall. (73 U.S.) 166 (1867); *Walkley* v. *City of Muscatine,* 6 Wall. (73 U.S.) 481 (1867); *Labette County Commissioners* v. *Moulton,* 112 U.S. 217 (1884); *County Commissioners of Cherokee County* v. *Wilson,* 109 U.S. 621 (1883). It would seem that the Virginia citations were little calculated to substantiate her point of view, for the relationship between the State and its creature, the municipality, is not analogous to that between the Union and the State.

[47] *Virginia* v. *West Virginia,* 246 U.S. 565, 599 (1918).

[48] *Ibid.*, p. 591, citing *Wayman* v. *Southard,* 10 Wheat. (23 U.S.) 1, 23 (1825); *Bank of the United States* v. *Halstead,* 10 Wheat. (23 U.S.) 51, 64 (1825); *Gordon* v. *United States,* 117 U.S. 697, 702 (1864). It may be noted that these cases involve suits between private individuals, and hence some question might arise as to their pertinency to the issue in the instant case.

[49] *Virginia* v. *West Virginia,* 246 U.S. 565, 600 (1918). [50] *Ibid.*, p. 601.

[51] *Ibid.*, p. 602. [52] *Ibid.*, p. 603.

[53] *Ibid.*, p. 604. [54] *Ibid.*

[55] *Ibid.*, p. 605.

[56] *Home Building & Loan Association* v. *Blaisdell,* 290 U.S. 398, 429 (1934), citing and quoting in part *Sturges* v. *Crowninshield,* 4 Wheat. (17 U.S.) 122, 197 (1819).

[57] "The Laws of the States and the Various Means for Bringing Them into Harmony." *State Government,* 9:116, June, 1936.

CHAPTER V

COOPERATIVE FEDERALISM: USES OF THE COMPACT

The uses for which resort has been made to the compact device are numerous and varied. Frankfurter and Landis, writing in 1925, found that the interstate compact had been used in connection with eight situations: boundaries and cessions of territory, control and improvement of navigation, penal jurisdiction, uniformity of legislation, interstate accounting, conservation of natural resources, utility regulation, and taxation.[1] It has been noted that, albeit the Compact Clause prior to 1934 afforded the basis for compacts designed to settle boundary disputes, to provide for construction of interstate public services, or to allocate the waters of interstate streams, since that time it has proved increasingly useful as a means of interstate cooperation in fields such as crime control, pollution abatement, allocation of oil production, conservation of fisheries resources, forest fire protection, flood control, and recreation as well.[2] To this list we may add civil defense and regional attacks upon deficiencies in educational facilities. These statements suffice to indicate that the uses of the compact device have indeed been increasingly varied. Published lists of compacts to which Congress has consented indicate, moreover, that the use of the device has been extensive.[3]

Boundaries and Cessions of Territory. The most frequent use of the compact device has been for the settlement of boundary disputes and the cession of territory. Compacts for this purpose have been negotiated throughout the history of the United States. As has been observed, "A boundary dispute may be designated as political in nature, best solved by joint fact-finding, and usually after much compromise; resort to litigation before the Supreme Court has in consequence generally proved less adequate than settlement through compact."[4] The Supreme Court has on occasion urged litigant States to resort to the compact method rather than suits to resolve their disagreements.[5] One such recommendation was made in the case of *Washington* v. *Oregon*[6] where the Court was asked to change and left unchanged the boundary line between those States. The boundary had been set originally as the center of the North Channel of the Columbia River subject to change by accretion, but the South Channel had developed into the more important one for navigational purposes.

Despite the demands of justice, the Court held that it was without "power to change the boundary" prescribed by Congress. The Court denied a petition for rehearing and recommended resort to compact to effect desirable or necessary change.[7] The extended use of the compact device for the settlement of this type of problem, and its efficacy as well, are attested by the fact that one commentator is able to brand the compact the "routine procedure for settling boundary disputes."[8] Numerous examples of this use might be cited, among them being the Virginia-Kentucky agreement of 1800, supplementing that of 1789; the Kentucky-Tennessee agreement of 1820; the Virginia-Maryland agreement of 1877; the 1909 agreements between Mississippi and Louisiana, Mississippi and Arkansas, and Tennessee and Arkansas; the Wisconsin-Minnesota agreement of 1917 effecting mutual cessions of territory and consequent changes of boundary; the Pennsylvania-Delaware agreement of 1921; the Missouri-Iowa agreement of 1939; the 1943 Indiana-Kentucky and Iowa-Nebraska agreements; the New York-Rhode Island agreement of 1944; and the Michigan, Minnesota, and Wisconsin agreement of 1948.

Crime Control. Various interstate agreements have been negotiated to establish jurisdiction of States over boundary waters. Such agreements are aimed at crime control. Examples are afforded by the 1909 agreements between Mississippi and Louisiana, Mississippi and Arkansas, and Tennessee and Arkansas with respect to the Mississippi River and the Oregon-Washington agreement of 1915 establishing the concurrent jurisdiction of those States over the Columbia River, primarily for the enforcement of laws regulating fishing.

Congress in 1910 granted its consent-in-advance to the States of Wisconsin, Illinois, Indiana, and Michigan, or any two of them, to make agreements not in conflict with the Constitution or laws of the United States "to determine and settle the jurisdiction to be exercised by said States, respectively, over offenses arising out of the violation of the laws of any of said States upon the waters of Lake Michigan."[9] Statement of this provision is enough to call to mind the difficulties inherent in the establishment of jurisdiction in such a case. M. Clifford Townsend, Governor of Indiana, indicated in an address to the National Conference on Interstate Trade Barriers that Lake Michigan had been a sort of "No Man's Land."

"The average citizen of the states surrounding the lake to say the least had a very hazy impression as to the ownership in, and jurisdiction over, Lake Michigan. The lake is not a Federal body of water and the Federal government has no more jurisdiction over Lake Michigan than it has over any other navigable water or interstate transportation system.

"While Lake Michigan is, in reality, an interstate body of water in which there has been since the creation of the surrounding states very definite although invisible boundaries, the haziness surrounding this conception unfortunately has been shared by public officials of these states for years." [10]

The Governor pointed out that steps had been taken to correct the situation through enactment of a uniform law by the individual States.

Agreements establishing jurisdiction of States over boundary waters, however, cover only one phase of interstate action for the control of crime. In 1934 Congress encouraged interstate cooperation against crime by granting its consent-in-advance "to any two or more states to enter into agreements or compacts for cooperative effort and mutual assistance in the prevention of crime and in the enforcement of their respective criminal laws and policies, and to establish such agencies, joint or otherwise, as they may deem desirable for making effective such agreements and compacts." [11] The congressional consent was in recognition of the fact that development of rapid means of transportation made enforcement of its criminal laws much more difficult for the individual State. [12] The encouragement bore fruit in the form of the most wide-spread agreement ever formulated by the States under the Compact Clause. It has been said that "With the single exception of the Constitution of the United States—an agreement among all the states, ratified by all the states—more of the states are signatories to the Interstate Compact for the Supervision of Parolees and Probationers than to any other formal agreement calling for coordinated effort and cooperative practices." [13] Since the time of that observation the forty-eighth State has become a party to the Parole-Probation Compact. [14] That 48 States ratified this compact calling for formal participation in a reciprocal program for supervising parolees and probationers is indeed a noteworthy achievement. Arrangements in the interest of crime control were made through cooperative uniform legislation or compacts covering interstate and intrastate fresh pursuit, extradition, out-of-state witnesses, interstate parole and probation supervision, law of arrest, firearms, and narcotic drugs. [15] The measure of successful control achieved under these arrangements is indicated by Mr. Joseph H. Hagan's observation that the "interstate 'commuting criminals' of the decade preceding the war, who took advantage of every legal device affording protection by state lines, were effectively stopped by a combination of federal-state enforcement machinery developed under a Uniform Crime Control Program." [16]

Interstate Accounting. The compact device has been employed once for interstate settlement of debt. This was the outgrowth of the creation of the State of West Virginia out of Virginia territory. Virginia consented to the separation on the basis of an agreement by which West Virginia obligated herself to assume an equitable proportion of the public debt of Virginia incurred while West Virginia was a part of that State. The precise amount of the indebtedness was determined, however, only after extended litigation in the Supreme Court.[17] The fact that the erection of new States from old ones does not appear on the horizon renders the particular form of interstate accounting effected by the Virginia-West Virginia compact not likely to arise in the near future.[18] But the compact may very well prove serviceable in the settlement of other interstate financial problems.

Uniform Legislation. In some fields uniformity of legislation among the several States is desirable and even necessary for the success of the programs of the individual States. The National Conference of Commissioners on Uniform State Laws, as its name implies, has directed its efforts toward such uniformity. And its achievements have been noteworthy in securing independent enactment by the States of identical laws. But a State may repeal one of its laws at will. Reliance has, therefore, at times been placed upon the Compact Clause to achieve uniformity and to assure its maintenance throughout the life of the compact. Furthermore, the risk which any particular State runs in taking unilateral action to establish minimum standards is evident. Industrial competition might, for example, take the form of increased hours of work and reduced wages in other States. A progressive State would run the risk of losing its industries to less progressive States or seeing its industries fail in competition with those of less progressive States. Nor is this particular danger restricted to the individual State. A regional interstate pact covering labor conditions in an industry might equally jeopardize the region and its industry. Thus, the cotton-textile industry could not be safeguarded by compact against internal competition of a cut-throat nature unless the New England cotton-textile States *and* those in the South adhered to the compact.

Proposals were made in the twenties that uniform state action in the labor field be secured through reciprocal statutes. But some question exists as to whether uniformity can be secured and maintained by means of a reciprocal statute which merely expresses a general mandate in the form of a minimum wage or a maximum work day and does not create some agency to convert that mandate into uniform specific regulations. The interstate compact implemented through a joint, continuous agency has been pointed to as the best device for the solution of such interstate difficulties.[19]

Representatives of the States of Connecticut, Maine, Massachusetts, New Hampshire, New York, Pennsylvania, and Rhode Island, on May 29, 1934, signed the Concord Compact, the first interstate compact "for Establishing Uniform Standards for Conditions of Employment, Particularly with Regard to the Minimum Wage."[20] The compact provided for a permanent interstate commission which was to consider any question arising on the part of one or more of the ratifying States concerning a matter involved in the compact or in any state law adopted in pursuance thereof and to make recommendations thereupon to commissions to be established in each of the participating States. The agreement was to be ratified by each State before it became binding on that State. Only the States of Massachusetts, New Hampshire, and Rhode Island ratified the agreement, and New Hampshire abrogated it in 1943, Massachusetts in 1945. Abrogation was based upon intervening developments in the form of federal legislation and court decisions which rendered the compact unnecesary.[21]

One disadvantage in the use of compacts to achieve the establishment of standards is the danger that standardization will result in an agreed minimum—something of a lowest common denominator. This danger was foreseen and an attempt made to forestall it in the Concord Compact's proviso "that nothing herein contained shall be construed as abrogating, repealing, modifying or interfering with the operation of laws already in effect in any State party hereto which establish standards equivalent to or above those herein specified, nor to prevent or discourage the enactment of additional laws establishing similar or higher standards; nor shall anything herein contained repeal or affect any laws concerning conditions of employment that are not in conflict herewith or that deal with subjects not included herein. . . ."[22]

Conservation and Use of Natural Resources. Under this general heading may be classed the conservation of natural resources, such as fish and marine life generally, oil, and forests, the apportionment of waters of interstate streams for reclamation and other uses, and the related problem of pollution control.

It was noted above under uniformity of legislation that the States bordering Lake Michigan attempted through enactment of a uniform law to place that "No Man's Land" under control. One aim of the States in undertaking this action was effective conservation of natural resources. The law was "aimed at the arresting of . . . wholesale destruction and expected to result in a replenishment of fish in marketable quantities during the coming years."[23] Indiana's Governor pointed to the "haziness" prevalent as to jurisdiction and asserted that "The result has been that fishing fleets have been permitted to operate ruthlessly and without any unified or effective control."[24] The fact that fish fail to recognize state boundary lines in boundary waters would render unilateral action fruitless. As Messrs. Frankfurter and Landis note, "Regional control is the practical answer to wasteful non-action or wasteful conflict. Vigilance by one State, though based on scientific direction, may be thwarted by inaction, or lax administration, in an adjoining State."[25] Alice Mary Dodd observes that "Conservation of food through the resort to state compacts is a challenge to the foresight and ingenuity of the states themselves."[26] She cites in support of her statement the observation of Francis C. Wilson that "Experience has taught us . . . that the representatives of the states in Congress will not, when subject to powerful executive pressure, protect the states from such attacks [as encroachments by Congress upon the reserved powers of the states]. The states, then, must assume the burden of their own defense."[27] The States are beginning to assume that burden finally, albeit they have been slow to do so. As early as 1785 two States—Virginia and Maryland—worked out an interstate arrangement for the protection of fish in boundary waters; but more often marine food resources have been reduced almost to the point of depletion before the interested States were stirred to conserve them, if they did so then.

One sees frequent newspaper items on the urgency of working out interstate protective arrangements covering this or that form of marine life. With respect to the Virginia-Maryland compact referred to above fifteen amendments have recently been suggested which would extend Virginia-Maryland joint control, now covering only oyster beds in the Tidewater Potomac, to all fisheries in the whole of Chesapeake Bay. The proposed amendments, which were drafted by a joint commission after public hearings in the two States, have been adopted by the Maryland Legislature but will not become effective until the Virginia General Assembly approves them.[28] The difficulty inherent in unilateral control was indicated in an editorial in the *Richmond Times-Dispatch*:

"Oysterbeds are comparatively static, but migratory fish and crabs are no respecters of State boundaries. Nor do the tides of the element in which they travel come to a halt at 'the dotted line.'

"The waters of the bay and the life it harbors are themselves of interstate character, a fact which makes joint, interstate control of their marine life a sensible and equitable arrangement."[29]

The editorial attitude of the *Richmond Times-Dispatch* toward extension is summed up in the observation that "our acceptance of the courtesy of joint control over the Maryland-owned Potomac all these years" would seem to impose upon us "a moral obligation to reciprocate at a time when Chesapeake Bay, in the opinion of competent biologists, must be similarly controlled."[30] But the creation of a bilateral Chesapeake seafood control commission embraced in the changes to the compact is both advocated and opposed.[31] At any rate, the 1950 Virginia General Assembly failed to concur in the 1949 Maryland Act for setting up a Chesapeake-Potomac Authority for the joint control or conservation of all seafood in the interstate area. The failure posed the question of whether Marylanders might agitate for unilateral repeal of the Compact of 1785.[32]

Other attempts at cooperative interstate action through compact to protect the fish supply would include the 1915 Oregon-Washington agreement to protect the salmon resources of the Coumbia River and the seaboard marine fisheries compacts.

Congress in 1940 granted its consent-in-advance to having the Atlantic States enter a compact to promote better utilization of marine, shell, and anadromous fisheries of the Atlantic Seaboard, and to establish the Atlantic States Marine Fisheries Commission. The outgrowth was the Atlantic States Marine Fisheries Compact, which by 1945 was ratified by all fourteen of the Atlantic Coast States and was approved by Congress in 1942. The intent of the compact was "the achievement of an effective, unified management of the fisheries of the Coastal states in order to prevent the depletion of one of the nation's important food sources."[33] The Secretary-Treasurer of the Commission, Mr. Wayne D. Heydecker, states that "The Commission represents a new concept of intergovernmental cooperation, a joint agency of many states working in close cooperation with federal technicians on programs which the states believe will benefit their respective fisheries. . . . Its officers believe the Atlantic States Marine Fisheries Commission, through its form of organization and method of operation, is demonstrating that results can be achieved even in so complicated a field as the coastal and migratory fisheries when men of good will from the several states are determined to accept their respective responsibilities and cooperate to fulfill them."[34] After its adoption the compact was amended to permit the States to establish joint regulation of common fisheries. At the end of 1951 eight States had ratified the amendment, and Congress had signified its assent to it. This constitutes a partial change in the advisory character of the Commission.[34a] This compact formed a precedent which led to the negotiation of compacts for other areas in the form of the Pacific States Marine Fisheries Compact and the Gulf States Marine Fisheries Compact.[35]

Conservation of oil resources has also been attempted by means of the interstate compact. This is another field in which unilateral action by one of the States would be ineffective. The 1935 report of the National Resources Committee briefly summarizes the factors preventing stabilization of the oil industry:

"One of these is the doctrine of capture which makes it legal for an oil operator to tap his neighbor's pools; the only possible redress for the neighbor is offset drilling—in other words, feverish competition for the market and resulting overproduction. Another factor is that of the 'flush pool,' which is demoralizing in its effect upon all attempts to effect a balance between supply and demand. The flush pool, wastefully operated, can produce oil for a time at far lower costs of production than the more settled fields; it thus performs the double function of waste and cut-throat competition. Individual States may stabilize their oil industries by proration or the limitation of production, and so avert within their borders the harmful effects of the doctrine of capture and the phenomenon of the flush pool. But, unless an interstate agreement is reached, flush pools from other States can ruin stabilization so secured by independent State action."[36]

To tackle this problem oil-producing States have joined together in the Interstate Oil Compact of 1935. By 1948 twenty-one States had signed this compact.[37] The compact governs the allocation of state petroleum production. Under the compact there was organized in 1935 the Interstate Oil Compact Commission, an agency "Dedicated to the Conservation of Oil and Gas," as its motto reads. Mr. Arthur S. Davenport, Assistant to the Secretary of the Commission, has said that the Commission "has for its sole purpose the promulgation of rules, regulations, and projects to conserve the nation's oil and gas by the prevention of physical waste."[38]

The National Resources Committee points out that the attempt to attack the evils of oil and gas wastage caused by competitive drilling raises some difficult questions. How is the consumer's interest to be protected? The consumer is opposed to waste but also opposed to the control of prices and distribution conditions so as to deprive him of the benefits of competition or consultation in the determination of policies. And what consideration is to be given to the complex interests of industrial workers who desire "an expansion of employment opportunities in the industry, of competing firms, and of the various communities dependent upon the industry?"[39] Finally, there are problems of enforcement both within the individual States and as among the States which pose real difficulties.

These questions serve to point up the fact that mere entry into an interstate compact is not an assurance of cure for all ills and the additional fact that interests must be weighed before the advisability of entering a compact such as that controlling oil production can be determined. Yet one analyst observes that the Oil Compact Commission "stands forth as perhaps the nation's most notable example of the success and practicability of the compact method in the solution of perplexing interstate problems. One of the greatest achievements of this interstate cooperative body has been that of instilling in the minds of the public and the various branches of the state and Federal governments, confidence in its aims and objectives, and general approval of the voluntary collaboration method in correlating divergent state views and opinions." [40]

Congress attempted in 1911 to spur interstate cooperative action in the field of forest conservation by passing the Weeks Act, authorizing "each of the several States of the Union to enter into any agreement or compact, not in conflict with any law of the United States, with any other State or States for the purpose of conserving the forests and the water supply of the States entering into such agreement or compact." [41] Congressional consent-in-advance failed to produce immediate action in this sphere. The problem meanwhile has grown more rather than less acute. The *Richmond Times-Dispatch* in a 1949 editorial advocates action by the lumbermen or the States as the only alternatives to action by Congress "in a belated attempt to forestall a timber famine." [42]

One aspect of the forest conservation problem is made the butt of attack in the Northeastern Interstate Forest Fire Protection Compact. Congress in 1949 [43] gave its consent and approval to this compact designed to promote effective forest fire prevention and control in the northeastern region of the United States and adjoining areas in Canada. The compact provides for maintenance of adequate fire-fighting services, mutual aid, and the establishment of a central coordinating agency, the Northeastern Forest Fire Protection Commission. The compact became operative as to the States which ratified it when adopted by any two or more of the States of Connecticut, Maine, Massachusetts, New Hampshire, New York, Rhode Island, and Vermont. All of those States have ratified it. [44] The compact is an "open" one in the sense that it provides that any State or any Canadian Province contiguous with one of the member States may become party to it: A proviso in the congressional act of approval stipulates that "before any province of the Dominion of Canada shall be made a party to such compact, the further consent of Congress shall first be obtained." [45] This compact has been termed "especially significant" in virtue of its international aspect, "laying the basis for agreement between the several states of the United

States and the provinces of Canada through the compact process rather than through the processes of treaty-making by negotiation between the United States and the Canadian national governments."[46]

Connected with forest depletion, partly in a cause-and-effect relationship, is the problem of flood control. Unilateral action on the part of a State to prevent flood damage would be effective only if the boundaries of the State coincided with those of the drainage basin. The interstate compact has been employed to permit treatment of the problem on the scale of the problem-area. One of the major purposes of the Colorado River Compact is to secure the "protection of life and property from floods."[47] The Red River Flood Control Compact, a 1937 agreement between Minnesota, North Dakota, and South Dakota dealing with flood control, utilization of waters, and prevention of pollution, and establishing a Tri-State Waters Commission, is another example of this type of compact.

In order to encourage this type of compact Congress in the Flood Control Act of 1936[48] granted its consent-in-advance "to any two or more States to enter into compacts or agreements in connection with any project or operation authorized by this Act for flood control or the prevention of damage to life or property by reason of floods upon any stream or streams and their tributaries, which lie in two or more such States. . . ."[49]

In 1949 four New England States, Connecticut, Massachusetts, New Hampshire, and Vermont, signed a pact providing for construction of twelve dams on the Connecticut River and establishing an interstate flood-control commission. By the close of 1951 all four of those States had ratified the Connecticut River Compact.[50]

Conservation of natural resources is closely related to reclamation of arid lands, an activity which places a premium upon the available water supply in the arid regions of the country. The problem of the apportionment of waters of interstate rivers is one the solution of which has occasioned frequent use of the compact device. Some indication of the extent of that use is afforded by listing the rivers involved in such attempts to arrive at equitable distribution. They would include the Colorado,[51] La Plata, Columbia, South Platte, Snake, Belle Fourche, Cheyenne, Rio Grande, Pecos, Canadian, Red, Gila, San Francisco, Arkansas, Yellowstone, Little Missouri, Republican, Costilla Creek, and Bear rivers. Most of the compacts or projected compacts embrace the tributaries of these rivers as well. The problem is one of vital concern to the interested areas. Mr. Justice Holmes pointed to this fact in the Delaware River case, when he observed that a river is a "treasure," and that it "offers a necessity of life that must be rationed among those who have power over it."[52] Of course the State closer to the source of the river has the physical power to cut off all the water within its jurisdiction. But, as Holmes pointed out, the exercise of such a power to the destruction of the interest of lower States clearly could not be tolerated. Equally the lower States could not be permitted to require the higher to refrain from cutting off any of the water in order that the river might come down undiminished. The substantial interests of all in the river must be reconciled as best they may be to achieve an equitable apportionment.[53]

Litigation has proved an unsatisfactory means of settling interstate difficulties anent pollution of streams. The problem of sewage disposal is one the solution of which has been met on several occasions by cooperative action through the compact method.[53a] As has been observed, when the courts attempt "to apply doctrines of riparian rights to interstate difficulties of this kind the central problem—which is legislative and administrative, rather than judicial—is left untouched."[54] The Supreme Court recognized the inherent inadequacy of courts in handling such problems satisfactorily when it suggested in *New York* v. *New Jersey*[55] that "the grave problem of sewage disposal presented by the large and growing populations living on the shores of New York Bay is one more likely to be wisely solved by cooperative study and by conference and mutual concession on the part of representatives of the States so vitally interested in it than by proceedings in any court however constituted." Yet the compact method can afford satisfactory solution of the pollution problem only if all the States whose lands form a part of the drainage basin cooperate. The reason is pointed out in an editorial dealing with the Ohio River Pollution Pact in which it is observed that "one polluted stream, like one bad apple in a barrel, can contaminate others which are unoffending, and for that reason the co-operation of all States abutting on the Ohio Valley is essential to the success of the effort."[56] Recognition of the fact that success for such a program is dependent upon the participation of all is indicated, in connection with the Ohio Pact, by Pennsylvania and Ohio making their acceptance contingent upon West Virginia's, and by West Virginia, in turn, making her acceptance subject to Virginia's. Moreover, Mr. Edwin R. Cotton, Engineer-Secretary of the Interstate Commission on the Potomac River Basin,[57] has observed that the Commission found the "use and conservation of all the natural resources . . . so interrelated that it must, of necessity, in planning a basin-wide pollution abatement program, consider and coordinate all plans for the use and conservation of natural resources of the area."[58] But the benefits which accrue to the area as a result of satisfactory solution of the pollution problem are manifold. Mr. James H. Allen lists those which would result in the Delaware watershed: "It will stimulate the use of the Delaware River as a highway of commerce. It will enhance the usefulness of the waters of the region for municipal and industrial water supply, the restoration of shad and other fish life, recreation, the protection of lower bay oyster industry, and many other purposes. It will improve working conditions along, and appreciate the value of, river front properties."[59] The return would seem to merit the effort. And the compact device affords a means whereby an agency can be created with a territorial scope of authority coterminous with the area of the problem to be met.

Taxation. Messrs. Frankfurter and Landis wrote in 1925 that "in view of the growing burden upon time and feelings, as well as the cost in money due to the conflicts and confusion arising from the administration of independent systems of State taxation, the possibilities of amelioration and economy realizable through an alert use of the Compact Clause call for more intensive study, as part of a disciplined attack upon the entire tax problem."[60] Few would deny the pertinency of the statement. But the States are exceedingly jealous of their taxing power and probably willing to compromise least of all with respect to it.

The Kansas City waterworks agreement of 1921 affords an example of the use of the compact device to prevent taxation of common resources. As it was deemed "vital to each city (Kansas City, Kansas, and Kansas City, Missouri) that each [waterworks] plant be free from assessment and taxation in the other State," the States of Kansas and Missouri with the consent of Congress entered a compact the substance of which was that Kansas should never "assess, levy, or collect any taxes, assessments, or imposts of any kind or character whatsoever on the portion of the waterworks plant of the municipality of Kansas City, Missouri, now or hereafter located within the territory of the State of Kansas" and that Missouri should reciprocate with respect to property of the Kansas City, Kansas, waterworks located within Missouri.[61] It would seem a little ludicrous that Congress should have to waste its time upon a matter which might better be left, perhaps, to local decision. But when a city spills over state lines, its governmental problems become interstate. Avoidance of possible duplicate taxation of, and provision for tax immunity for, such governmental property as the municipal waterworks involved in the Kansas-Missouri compact can be achieved and more or less "frozen" by incorporation into an interstate compact.

A somewhat different type of benefit accrual of which has been anticipated from interstate agreement is elimination of tax evasion. One of the advantages to be derived from a "hoped for" Great Lakes Authority to be patterned after the Port of New York Authority was said to be that such an authority would furnish a means whereby

". . . the Great Lakes states, collectively, could end the present evasion of taxation on the part of Great Lakes commercial vessels. Most of these vessels, totaling millions of dollars in taxable property, now escape taxation by any of the states between which they ply in interstate commerce by registering out of ports of Delaware which it is doubtful the vessels could reach even under calm conditions on the Atlantic, and which the vessels have never touched and to which they never will put in. By a unified approach, the Lake states through such an Authority could require a registry and tax situs at the home port of each vessel on the lake." [62]

The important element is the "unified approach," and the compact device affords a means whereby it can be achieved.

Control and Improvement of Navigation. Even before adoption of the Constitution the interests of adjoining States in common waters led them to negotiate agreements controlling navigation and use of such waters. [63] Those interests continued after adoption of the Constitution and caused resort to the Compact Clause by the States to cope with the difficulties posed. The best-known result is the 1921 agreement between New York and New Jersey establishing the Port of New York Authority, which was characterized in 1935 as "perhaps the most important regional administrative agency yet developed." [64]

The Port of New York is an organic whole from the "point of view of geography, commerce, and engineering," while, politically, it is "split between the law-making of two States, independent but futile in their respective spheres." [65] Many municipalities are located on the banks of the Hudson, and they had "sought to satisfy their interest in the general problem through a confusion of local regulations." The United States also had asserted its power to "regulate Commerce with foreign Nations, and among the several States." Messrs. Frankfurter and Landis neatly summarize the situation in their observation that "What in fact was one, in law was many." [66]

The situation called for and was met by concerted action of New York, New Jersey, and the United States. That action took the form of the compact of 1921 which created the Port of New York Authority, an interstate administrative agency, and empowered it to "purchase, construct, lease and/or operate any terminal or transportation facility within said district; and to make charges for the use thereof; and for any of such purposes to own, hold, lease and/or operate real or personal property, to borrow money and secure the same by bonds or by mortgages upon any property held or to be held by it."[67] The Authority was made the principal planning agency for the development of the Port and was entrusted with the administration of its plans "when such plans are duly approved by the legislatures of the two states."[68] The Authority's activities through the years since its inception have been such that it has been considered eminently successful as a business enterprise and something less than successful as a planning agency. In 1933 it was termed "a poor but honest corporation which failed to the tune of a $175,000,000 success, with a $10,000,000 income for the year 1932 and $20,000,000 liquid assets in the bank."[69] Its outstanding success was in the construction and operation of bridge and tunnel facilities. One factor which should be noted with respect to this success, the National Resources Committee points out, is the "concentration of population in and about the port of New York which assures a steady and large use of the facilities which the authority provides and thereby simplifies the problem of financing such public works from current income. . . ."[70] The Authority is significant, from the standpoint of governmental administration and planning, as additional evidence that the government corporation affords the government an efficient device for operating government-owned economic enterprises.[71]

The National Resources Committee maintains that the compact method is ill-adapted to the planning function when the problem is a continuing and complex one. The conclusion would seem to be dependent upon the powers afforded the agency. It is certain that the Authority lacked the power to compel compliance with its plan on the part of the interstate railroads. And the actions of the latter lend weight to the Committee's observation that, "When valuable interests such as water rights and transportation facilities are the subject matter of distribution or development, clashes of interest, attempts to forestall, all manner of interferences and obstructions may be expected."[72] The blame for the failure of the Authority's original comprehensive plan, it has been said, must rest primarily upon the refusal of the railroads to cooperate and upon the refusal of the Interstate Commerce Commission to force the railroads to cooperate.[73] There would seem, however, to be something to the appraisal of an "unsuccessful instrument of government which, deprived of its powers by court decisions and cheated of its purpose by the obstructionism of individuals, nevertheless finds a related field of service and a roundabout way of approaching the original goal" as "something new and unheard-of under the political sun."[74] Perhaps it is too early finally to evaluate the planning activities of the Authority.

If regional planning and economic development are considered the dominant characteristics of the New York-New Jersey compact, the Colorado River Compact and the Missouri-Illinois Development Compact are comparable to it. The "major purposes" of the Colorado River Compact are declared to be "to provide for the equitable division and apportionment of the use of the waters of the Colorado River system; to establish the relative importance of different beneficial uses of water; to promote interstate comity; to remove causes of present and future controversies; and to secure the expeditious agricultural and industrial development of the Colorado River Basin, the storage of its waters, and the protection of life and property from floods."[75] The National Resources Committee notes that the second major purpose, that of establishing the relative importance of different beneficial uses of water, "has a direct bearing on the manner in which developments on the river may proceed."[76] Navigation uses are subordinated in importance by the compact to agricultural and domestic uses and to power uses, which, in that order, occupy the preferred positions.

The 1949 Missouri-Illinois compact provides for the establishment of a bi-state agency for the development of the St. Louis metropolitan area with authority to plan, construct, and operate bridges, tunnels, airports, and terminals, and to submit to the communities involved plans for the coordination of "streets, highways, parking areas, terminals, water supply and sewage and drainage facilities, land-use patterns, and other matters in which joint or coordinated action will be generally beneficial."[76a] The metropolitan district defined by the compact covers roughly 3,000 square miles and embraces approximately 225 municipalities and 750 local taxing districts with a population of 1,750,000—an adequate laboratory indeed.

Utility Regulation. Although Congress possesses plenary power to regulate interstate commerce and, for the most part, has chosen to exercise it with respect to the increasingly national system of transportation, there remains a considerable and important sphere of interstate communications predominantly regional in their importance. Much of this, Congress has seen fit not to regulate, both because it is more of local or regional significance than national and because national supervision would be excessively burdensome and ineffective.[77] Regulation to be effective must be by unified action on the part of the governments of the States comprising the affected region. And the compact affords a procedural device whereby that unified action can be, and has been achieved. An early example of resort to the compact device for this purpose is afforded by the agreement between Virginia, the District of Columbia, Maryland, and Pennsylvania with respect to the construction of a canal.[78] More recent examples of such use are afforded by the 1919 New York-New Jersey agreement for the construction of a tunnel under the Hudson River, the 1921 Kansas-Missouri agreement for the development of waterworks plants at Kansas City, the 1927 and 1935 New York-Vermont agreements for the construction of a bridge across Lake Champlain and the creation of a Lake Champlain Bridge Commission, and the 1937 Maine-New Hampshire agreement for creation of the Maine-New Hampshire Interstate Bridge Authority with power to construct, maintain, and operate a bridge between Portsmouth and Kittery.

Local privately-owned utilities usually are no respecters of state lines and consequently often pose real problems of regulation. The compact affords a compromise between extreme centralization of control and ineffective regulation through individual state action.

Civil Defense. In the period following World War II thoughts of the probable effects of atomic attack precipitated a new outlook upon civil defense. The concern was no longer couched in terms of the family unit, the block, or the city, but rather was one of how to keep the country as a whole a going concern. Comprehensive intra-state and interstate mutual aid programs between political units were worked out. The interstate compact afforded the legal basis for regional defense organization. At the close of 1950, eleven States had made specific provision for regional defense plans, four more permitted cooperation on the part of peripheral counties and cities with adjacent counties and cities of neighboring States, and four other States authorized regional defense organizations for "critical" areas.[79]

In September of 1950 Governor Thomas E. Dewey of New York and Governor Alfred E. Driscoll of New Jersey signed a mutual aid agreement which the New Jersey Civil Defense Director termed a "long step forward in interstate cooperation" and a likely "pattern for the entire United States."[80] The terms of this agreement indicate the "stuff" of such compacts. Under the New York-New Jersey agreement mutual aid includes "evacuation and reception of injured and homeless persons, as well as the exchange of medical, fire, police, public utility, reconnaissance, welfare, transportation and communications personnel, equipment, supplies, and such additional services and facilities as shall be necessary."[81] Provision is made, also, for development of "detailed agreements and plans for mutual military aid" in support of civil defense. Mutual aid apparently strikes the States as suited to the civil defense need.

Ten States in the Northeastern region have completed action to participate in a regional uniform civil defense and disaster compact.[82] Moreover, the Northeastern regional compact has served as a model for States in other regions of the country. Basic agreement has been reached by seven Western States in two mutual assistance compacts. In the one Arizona, Colorado, Kansas, New Mexico, Oklahoma, and Texas are participants, while the other embraces the States of Arizona, Colorado, New Mexico, and Utah.[83] California, Oregon, and Washington defense officials have approved an interstate Pacific Coast defense compact for their States,[84] and other States are in the legislative throes of empowering their governors to sign mutual aid compacts which probably will be forthcoming. The compacts made and to be made in this field add up to one more use of the compact device.

Regional Education. Southern interest in regional advanced educational institutions was precipitated in part by the Supreme Court decision in the *Gaines* case.[85] Gaines, a fully qualified Negro, was refused admission to the law school of the University of Missouri on the ground that it was "contrary to the constitution, laws and public policy of the state to admit a negro as a student in the University of Missouri." Missouri law provided for payment of tuition fees for Negro students, residents of the State of Missouri, in adjacent state universities admitting non-resident Negroes. The state universities of Kansas, Nebraska, Iowa, and Illinois maintained law schools to which non-resident Negroes were admitted. The Missouri supreme court affirmed a judgment denying a writ of mandamus to compel the curators of the University of Missouri to admit Gaines; but the United States Supreme Court on certiorari reversed the state court decision, holding that Missouri's failure to provide a law school within its bounds for Negro residents while providing one for white students constituted a denial of equal protection of the laws in violation of the Fourteenth Amendment of the Constitution. The holding was not a rejection of the *Plessy* v. *Ferguson*[86] rule that segregation of the races does not in itself deny equal protection if the accommodations accorded the two races are equal. But the Court did say that the "admissibility of laws separating the races in the enjoyment of privileges afforded by the State rests wholly upon the equality of the privileges which the laws give to the separated groups within the State."[87] The out-of-state subsidy plan was dealt a telling blow by the Court in its holding that the "obligation of the State to give the protection of equal laws can be performed only where its laws operate, that is, within its own jurisdiction."[88] That obligation the Court deemed imposed by the Constitution upon the States severally, and hence the burden of the obligation could not be "cast by one State upon another." The State of Missouri was "bound to furnish him [Gaines] within its borders facilities for legal education substantially equal to those which the State there afforded for persons of the white race. . . ."[89]

It is obvious that the *Gaines* decision greatly increased the urgency of the need for providing new and extending old educational facilities. Governor Jim Nance McCord of Tennessee suggested to the Governors assembled at the Conference of Southern Governors at Asheville, North Carolina, in October of 1947, that the Southern States consider the possibilities of cooperative action through compacts in the provision of educational facilities, particularly those for Negroes. The problem exists only on the level of advanced instruction, for the States maintain tax-supported colleges offering Negroes courses leading to the bachelor's degree, and those colleges meet the requirement of equal facilities essential to satisfaction of the Constitution's equal protection clause.

The alternatives open to the Southern States, in the face of the *Gaines* decision, Governor McCord saw as three: (1) to close the professional schools now maintained by the States, thereby denying educational opportunities in this field to white and colored students alike; (2) to eliminate segregation, thus permitting white and colored students to attend existing professional schools on a basis of equality; and (3) to establish professional schools for Negroes, affording them facilities and training substantially equal to those offered to whites.[90] Governor McCord rejected the first two of these alternatives as impractical. He observed that Southern States "certainly cannot abandon . . . existing facilities for professional education" and yet, if the alternative of admitting Negro students along with white students were to be adopted, those facilities "might as well be abandoned as such action would effectively destroy the operation of our professional schools." The effect of eliminating segregation in existing tax-supported professional schools can only be conjectured, but Governor McCord's conjecture probably would represent the view of a large segment of the population in the States imposing segregation. Senator Langer observed in a later debate in the Senate that the white pupils of the Universities of Texas and Oklahoma recently "voted by an overwhelming majority that they wish to have colored students admitted; that they wish to associate with them; that they wish to have them there."[91] Senator Wiley, commenting on Langer's statement, said that "there is a light in the darkness" but pointed out also that "we are a government of majorities."[92] Both of Senator Wiley's points would seem well taken. The only really practical course of the three alternatives is, according to Governor McCord's conclusions, the third, *i.e.*, provision of facilities for Negroes equal to those provided for whites.

The Southern Governors at their 1947 conference in Asheville, North Carolina, adopted by unanimous vote a resolution calling upon Congress to authorize the Southern States' entry into compacts for the establishment of regional educational facilities. At a subsequent Southern Governors' Conference in Tallahassee, Florida, in 1948, the States of Alabama, Arkansas, Florida, Georgia, Maryland, Mississippi, South Carolina, Tennessee, and Texas entered into a "compact relating to the establishment of a Board of Control for Southern Regional Education, providing for the planning, establishment, acquisition, and operation of educational institutions on a regional basis, supported by public funds derived from taxation by the constituent States, in accordance with the terms, provisions, and conditions set out and contained in said compact. . . ."[93] Following this conference Southern representatives introduced resolutions designed to grant the consent of Congress to this compact, but the resolutions were buried in a Senate Committee.[94]

The basis for a regional approach to the problem of providing the needed facilities is two-fold: the Southern States are financially unable individually to make such provision or would be heavily burdened in doing so; and no single Southern State has sufficient demand on the part of qualified Negroes to warrant establishment and maintenance of such schools.[95] By use of the compact "Several States could much more readily pool their resources, and thus provide not only instruction, but instruction of the very best grade."[96] The "regional approach" has been advocated as "eminently sensible from the standpoint of *both* whites and Negroes in the South" and as a means of providing needed facilities for each of the races.[97] Yet, a news item telling of the compact's approval by the Senate Judiciary Committee records that, "Although it is not specified in the agreement, present plans call for primary emphasis on medical, dental, law and other professional graduate schools for Negroes who are not admitted to the all-white State universities of the South."[98]

Segregation was certainly made an issue in the Senate debate on the regional school compact.[99] Speaking against the Morse anti-segregation amendment, Senator Elbert D. Thomas of Utah said:

"Under present circumstances and under the present laws of these States and the law of the land, and in view of what the States are trying to do under the instructions set forth in decisions rendered by the Supreme Court of the United States, that would be unwise, and it would bring about the very opposite of what we are trying to do. . . .

"[There are those who] think the principle [of nonsegregation] is just and right, as I do; but everything cannot be done overnight. When at last the Southern States are entering into an agreement among themselves. . . , we know a new day is dawning. . . . The way to solve these [race] questions is not to stand absolutely on a principle which cannot be successfully made dominant in our generation, or perhaps in two or three generations, but to go forward as we have gone forward since the Civil War, doing the best possible under the circumstances." [100]

A Southern editorialist, commenting on Senator Thomas' statements, admitted the obligation of providing educational opportunity for the Negro but asserted that to "attempt overnight to destroy by statute the customs and beliefs which two centuries have implanted in a section embracing many millions of people will fail and will bring woe to both races." [101] The editorialist observed also that a "disturbing feature" of the prolonged Senate debate was the "introduction of messages from many Negro leaders which made it plain that those Negroes were not interested in higher educational opportunities for their race unless they could be had by admixture with whites." [102] If a purely conjectural note may be injected, it might indeed be true that the only way in which the Negro can achieve that sense of equality which may be essential to true "equality of facilities" is through elimination of segregation. [103] But statistics mustered in the Senate debate proved that, with facilities below demand, the number of Negroes admitted to medical schools, for example, would have been smaller, if Howard University and Meharry Medical College had not shown preference in admitting Negro students even though their qualifications were lower than those of white applicants and of the national average for medical students. In substance, segregation worked to the advantage of the Negroes in this case and might be expected to do so until the race could be brought up to a competitive level. This fact prompted Senator Sparkman to observe that a "great many of the so-called or would-be friends of the Negroes fight these windmills of segregation even at the expense of denying to the Negro a chance to break through . . . economic segregation. While fighting against segregation they deny to him an economic opportunity and a chance to get on and to make something out of his life." [104] Senator Sparkman pointed out, moreover, that more was involved in the compact than merely the establishment and maintenance of schools for giving Negroes higher education. "Of course," he said, "we hope that by the compact we shall be able to do a great deal more for the Negroes than we have ever done for them before, but by the same token we hope that we may be able to do a great deal more in our section of the country for the white boys and girls, as well as for the black boys and girls who want higher education and specialized training."[105]

It was argued in the Senate, on the one hand, that this was a compact on a matter which did not concern the United States and, hence, that it did not require the consent of Congress for its validity, and on the other hand, that all compacts required the consent of Congress for their validity. A third argument was advanced that the consent of Congress to the compact was not essential to its validity, but it was advisable for practical reasons to forestall suits to test validity on that score. Senator Wiley maintained that, since this was a compact for which consent was not necessary but merely advisable, Congress might not constitutionally impose conditions, and hence the proposed anti-segregation amendment should be rejected and, if adopted, would not bind the States. Senator Hatch briefly stated what would seem the most practical view with regard to the argument over the necessity of congressional consent.

"There is undoubtedly a strong view on the part of some, especially from the States which have proposed the compact, that a compact is necessary, and that it is necessary, under the Constitution, to have the consent of Congress. There is . . . evident difference of opinion. Assuming that such consent is unnecessary, that difference could never be resolved and determined until the courts had judicially passed upon a case in which, for instance, a taxpayer of the State of Florida sought to enjoin the use of tax money for the support of an institution in another State. . . . then it would have to go through a long process . . . to determine the question. If the contention be correct that the consent of Congress is unnecessary, what harm could arise from giving consent now? If it should prove to be necessary, grave injury could be done by denying consent. . . ."[106]

The final outcome of the Senate debate was a vote adverse to the proponents of consent for the compact in that the measure was referred to the Committee on the Judiciary. Representative Hobbs, addressing the House, observed that for the first time in the Nation's history an interstate compact had "been killed." He congratulated the House for having so overwhelmingly (236 to 45) given its consent to the regional education compact and noted that the Senate killed it by a vote of 38 to 37. The uniqueness of the Senate's action was highlighted by the observation that "One hundred and one of 102 compacts have been granted the consent of Congress."[107]

Editorialist Wright Bryan, writing in the *Atlanta Journal,* records disagreement among constitutional lawyers "as to whether congressional approval is necessary for this type of agreement among the states" with the "majority of them" seeming to think "that the states can proceed safely without any authority from Congress."[108] Senator Morse pointed to the Virginia-West Virginia agreement for West Virginia's use of a Richmond educational institution and the Vermont-New Hampshire agreement for joint use of a penitentiary as precedents for not approving the compact.[109]

The failure of Congress to grant its consent to the compact has been no deterrent to the Southern States. Those States have proceeded with their plans in the face of two adverse possibilities: (1) the courts might hold the compact one which requires the consent of Congress for its validity and thus invalid; and (2) the courts might hold the regional schools for Negroes no counterweight to those provided within the States for whites and hence inadequate to satisfy the equal protection clause of the Fourteenth Amendment.[110]

Shortly after the Southern Governors' Conference in Asheville adopted its resolution, the National Association for the Advancement of Colored People avowed its belief that "no State will be able to satisfy the requirements of the Fourteenth Amendment by setting up regional areas while retaining separate and individual Statewide universities for white students. . . . The NAACP fight for complete equality of education opportunities will continue."[111] The Southern States apparently may rest assured of an opportunity to learn whether the proposed regional school arrangement will satisfy the requirements of the Fourteenth Amendment.

Governor McCord thought it might "reasonably be argued" that such a plan afforded the colored student equal protection. "There is quite a difference," he said, "between the mere furnishing of a scholarship in an institution in some distant State and the creation of a regional district where each State is the joint proprietor and joint operator of a regional school established by State compacts specifically authorized by the Federal Constitution."[112] According to the language of the proposed compact, "the said several States do hereby form a geographical district or region consisting of the areas lying within the boundaries of the contracting States which, for the purposes of this compact, shall constitute an area for regional education supported by public funds derived from taxation by the constituent States for the establishment, acquisition, operation, and maintenance of regional educational schools and institutions for the benefit of citizens of the respective States residing within the region so established as may be determined from time to time in accordance with the terms and provisions of this compact."[113] The State thus enlarges its jurisdiction. Whether creation of this new educational jurisdiction would be held to satisfy the individual State's obligation to provide "substantially equal" facilities for colored students "within its own jurisdiction" and "within its borders"[114] is largely conjectural. One commentator observed:

"It appears that if the Supreme Court adhered strictly to the *Gaines* decision, it would hold as a matter of law that regional colleges do not meet the equal protection requirements there laid down. But social sentiment in the South among whites is apparently still unwilling to abandon segregation in education; and the financial inability of Southern states to provide separate professional graduate facilities is probably undeniable. A majority of the Court, therefore, might take recognition of these practical factors. If convinced that the regional college project was a sincere effort to reconcile all the difficulties—legal, social and economic—in a troublesome situation, the Court could distinguish the *Gaines* subsidy plan from the regional approach and uphold the latter as meeting equal protection standards."[115]

An editorial writer for the *Richmond Times-Dispatch* points out that at the time the *Gaines* decision was rendered the "regional concept" was not being widely discussed and observes, perhaps optimistically, that now that the regional school plan "has been proposed for both whites and Negroes, the court might take a different view."[116] The courts might well be influenced by the practical aspects of the situation to give the Southern States an opportunity to prove good faith.

A *New York Times* editorial voices what might prove a deterrent to doctrinaire opposition by colored organizations and indeed to doctrinaire reasoning by members of the Supreme Court.

"Educational pragmatists among Negro educators will support the . . . case for the Southern regional college [*sic*] plan (initiated without the blessing of a Congressional compact) because of its definite gain for Negro education. A mere token compliance of Southern state universities with the letter of the Supreme Court's rulings that would admit a few Negroes would not supply Negro professionals in the numbers needed. The . . . plan pledges higher education for the Negro under a program that promises legislative support for a considerable period. While essential features of the plan may be distasteful to a representative segment of American opinion, because of its practical values it is not likely to be discarded until a maturing sense of public responsibility for Negro education offers something better."[117]

The editorial points out, however, that the regional college solution of the South's Negro problem "may have to face the legal objection that the logic by which it proposes to meet the Supreme Court's directive to every State to provide equal educational facilities by a collective effort to furnish them to most Negro students beyond the borders of their State, is tortured and will not stand the constitutional test. There is also a thoughtful group, including members of both races, which believes that the place to begin to break down the barriers of segregation in American democracy is at the level of graduate education, which represents a peak of enlightenment."

It has been suggested that, even if the Court holds the regional school system inadequate to satisfy equal protection requirements so long as white state universities are maintained, it need not mean the program's demise. "One solution would be to place all professional schools in the South on a regional basis. . . . This would remove all question as to the equality of opportunity provided by the states, save for the possible question arising from the variations in the distances which a particular student would have to travel to reach his segregated school." [118]

Florida's Governor Millard Caldwell, as chairman of the Board of Control for Southern Regional Education, pointed out that a court decision to the effect that the educational facilities made available under the regional compact do not satisfy the requirement of the Fourteenth Amendment for substantial equality in facilities for white and colored students "relates only to a specific use of regional activities, not to the validity of the regional compact itself or to the validity of regional arrangements for all groups of citizens within a State." [119] The aim of the Board, he stated, is the improvement and expansion of available educational opportunities "for the training of all the youth of the South within the framework of the law. It is hoped that no effort will be made to use the provision of facilities so offered as a defense to any legal action." He stated further than the "plan is not intended to relieve the States of any responsibility under the fourteenth amendment of the United States Constitution, nor can it, for that matter. If given a chance, regional planning will surely assist States, institutions, and agencies concerned with higher education in their efforts to advance knowledge and improve the social and economic level of the southern region."

When Esther McCready, a Negro applicant for admission to the University of Maryland's school of nursing, was refused admission, the University Board of Regents advanced the contention that it was providing "equal facilities" under the regional program at Meharry Medical College in Tennessee. The Regional Board of Control intervened, observing that the program was not intended to serve any State "as a legal defense for avoiding responsibilities established under the existing State and Federal laws and court decisions." The Maryland

Court of Appeals decided in favor of the applicant, directing issuance of a writ of mandamus to require the University authorities' consideration of her application. The Supreme Court of the United States refused to grant certiorari, "thereby in effect," as the Regional Board's *Report* puts it, "sustaining the Board's position."[119a]

Meanwhile the Southern States have proceeded with plans for developing graduate, professional, and highly specialized types of educational facilities on a regional basis.[120] A Regional Council for Education, including representatives from fourteen Southern and border States, was set up and has been reconstituted as the Board of Control for Southern Regional Education. Millard Caldwell announced in late 1948 that some regional institutions would be ready to open in September of 1949.[120a] By June of 1949 contracts had been signed with nine medical, dental and veterinary medical colleges, but forty contracts were said to be expected soon.[121] One editorial identifies some of the nine institutions:

"The Medical College of Virginia, Louisiana State University, Emory University and Vanderbilt University have just signed contracts in Atlanta, under which they will offer medical and dental training to students from areas which do not offer it. Similarly the University of Georgia has made training in veterinary medicine available to Virginia students, and VPI has arranged to send 12 Virginians there. The institutions offering medical and dental training will be paid $1,500 a year by the States for each student trained by them, while $1,000 will be paid the University of Georgia by the State of Virginia and the others for each veterinary student."[122]

In January of 1950 it could be said that some forty contracts had been signed by the Board, the States, and the institutions defining regional arrangements in three fields—medicine, dentistry, and veterinary medicine. In the Fall semester of 1949, 388 students were enrolled under those contracts. Services in veterinary medicine are being provided by Alabama Polytechnic Institute, the University of Georgia, Oklahoma Agricultural and Mechanical College, and Tuskegee Institute. Six universities are providing dental training: Emory, Loyola of Louisiana, Maryland, Meharry Medical College, Tennessee, and the Medical College of Virginia. Seven afford services in medical training: Duke, Emory, Louisiana State, Meharry, Tennessee, Tulane, and Vanderbilt.[123]

At the start of the school year of 1949 there were regional contracts for 388 students, of whom slightly over half were white. The figures increased in the following year to 402 white and 182 Negro students, for a total of 584. In the fall of 1951, places were provided at 19 institutions for 850 students, 583 of whom were white and 267 Negro. There were 300 students enrolled in medicine, 265 in veterinary medicine, 250 in dentistry, and 35 in social work.[124] With respect to segregation it has been pointed out that "The school's own rules of segregation govern the students to be admitted."[125]

It is encouraging that the South has gone ahead with its plan to provide higher educational facilities for the Negro on a regional basis. Given the economic condition and prejudices of the South, the States of the region have stepped out on the only avenue open to them which can spell better educational opportunity for the Negro. It would be unfortunate, however, if the program were stigmatized as one designed solely to circumvent judicial attacks upon substantial inequalities in the existent segregated higher educational system. The current predominance of white over colored students calls into question such a characterization of the program. The potentialities of regional education warrant more considerate treatment. The Southern States have opened new vistas for the use of the compact device. Dr. John E. Ivey, Jr. and Dr. William J. McGlothlin, director and associate director, respectively, for the Board of Control for Southern Regional Education, point out that the program is accomplishing its immediate aim:

"It is providing education for students to whom the education was in most cases unavailable before the program was created. But above and beyond that, it is involving the institutions of the South in a forceful union that holds the promise of development to a greater goal: the building of a higher educational system based on the region's needs, a system which will help expand the region's resources, human and material, to a productive-and use-level never before equaled by any region of the Nation. Today it is only a hope, but a realistic one. The important thing is that the beginning has been made."[126]

Pooling of resources permits the greatest educational benefit to the region from the limited sums available for educational purposes. A State makes up its deficiencies in one field by borrowing the school of a neighbor State and underwrites the deficiency of its neighbor in another field. The system results in more efficient use of facilities and permits combination for the greater development of the institution promising greatest service to the region because of its location or other factors. Tennessee's Governor Gordon Browning points out that the search is not for "economy" as such but for the wisest and most ingenious expenditures *sans* waste and discouragement involved in useless duplication. "Through joint planning and joint effort . . . we can make our increasing investments in education serve more and more effectively to meet our needs."[127] Regional development and state development advance hand in hand, and the whole process adds up to a gain for the nation.

The Southern States are not alone in finding financially burdensome the provision and maintenance of educational institutions required for their citizens' professional and graduate training. The New England and the Western States have also developed cooperative programs in the realm of higher education.[128]

In the West, in particular, the financial burden has been great, for populations are widely scattered over considerable territorial expanses in part devoid of the large metropolitan areas which alone present the conditions necessary for some types of professional training. Critical areas such as those of medical and dental training precipitated the thought that an interstate cooperative attack might prove fruitful. The Southern Regional Education arrangements afforded a pattern.

At its 1949 meeting the Western Governors' Conference[129] endorsed the idea of Western cooperative regional education for the provision of more extensive facilities for training the region's students.[130] A technical advisory committee was formed and developed a regional education plan which was drawn up in compact form. The Western Governors' Conference unanimously approved the compact in November of 1950.

The compact provides for the creation of the Western Interstate Commission for Higher Education and stipulates that it is first to "endeavor to provide adequate services and facilities in the fields of dentistry, medicine, public health, and veterinary medicine, and may undertake similar activities in other professional and graduate fields." For this purpose the Commission was empowered to enter into contractual agreements. By its terms the compact becomes operative with respect to those adopting it when ratified by five States or Territories within the region. In May of 1951 Oregon afforded the necessary fifth-state ratification to bring it into effect. Colorado, Montana, New Mexico, and Utah previously had ratified it.[131]

The regional education compact affords tremendous potentialities for rich States and poor States alike. By resort to it any group of States can realize better utilization of the resources at hand and attainment of heights unattainable to any of its members acting alone.

Such are the uses which have been made of the interstate compact. What may be said about those uses for which it has been proposed?

Proposed Uses of the Compact Device. The possibilities of resort to the Compact Clause have been said to be "unlimited." Use of the device has been suggested to achieve regulation of interstate transportation, more particularly of motor trucks and vehicles travelling interstate, of air traffic, of child labor, and of public health; to standardize commodities, taxes (such as those imposed upon corporations, income, inheritance, gasoline, and liquor), and legislation (such as that covering divorce); and to solve problems in connection with taxing mail order houses and instituting programs for relief, public works, social security, unemployment insurance, drought and flood control, pest eradication, health and sanitation, and timber and game preservation. The list is by no means exhaustive. Miss Alice Dodd says that these and "many other purely interstate and sectional questions could be adjusted by the use of compacts insuring mutual interstate accord coupled with federal acquiescence in accordance with the Constitution."[132]

Cooperative attacks by the States are deemed both possible and feasible with respect to the facilitation and management of migratory farm labor and the administration of unemployment compensation in our fluid labor market.[133]

Miss Dodd, writing in 1936, recorded that some years prior to that time the States of New Hampshire and Vermont made provision for a joint penitentiary to serve both States, and observed that, if this might be done, "it would seem feasible that two or more states could join together for the purpose of consolidating their educational systems, including their state universities, the underlying advantage being economy and the raising of educational standards."[134] More recently the compact device has been seriously considered as affording a possible means whereby States might unite in the provision of advanced instruction. That consideration has resulted in the removal of interstate or regional education compacts from the category of "proposed uses" to that of "uses." The principle is available for transfer to other service fields. The possibilities of its adaptation in the provision of institutions for the correction of mental defectives and delinquent groups including alcoholics and sex offenders, and for the care of infants under three years of age are currently under consideration.[135]

[1] Frankfurter and Landis, "The Compact Clause of the Constitution," pp. 695-96. [2] *The Book of the States, 1950-51,* 8:23.

[3] *State Government,* 9:118-21, June, 1936, contains a list of compacts negotiated between 1789 and 1936, totalling 69 in number. This list is brought up through 1949 in *The Book of the States, 1950-51,* 8:26-31, where interstate compacts from 1934 through 1949 are listed in chronological order with name, subject, state ratification, consent of Congress (date and citation) given. The latter list contains 31 compacts, some of which were incomplete at the time of listing. In *The Book of the States, 1952-53,* 9:23-24, new ratifications and amendments to

existing interstate compacts for the years 1950-51 are given. A list of the acts by which Congress consented to or ratified the agreements prior to 1934 is to be found in the *Congressional Record,* Vol. 79, pt. 10, pp. 11344-45, July 17, 1935.

[4] National Resources Committee, *op. cit.,* p. 36.

[5] See ch. I, footnote 19, this study. [6] 211 U.S. 127 (1908).

[7] 214 U.S. 205, 218 (1909). See *supra,* Ch. I.

[8] See "Some Legal and Practical Problems of the Interstate Compact." *Yale Law Journal,* 45:325, December, 1935.

[9] 36 United States *Statutes at Large* 882.

[10] M. Clifford Townsend, "A State and Interstate Cooperation." *The Proceedings of the National Conference on Interstate Trade Barriers, April 5, 6, 7, 1939, Chicago, Illinois* (Chicago: The Council of State Governments, 1939), p. 87.

[11] 48 United States *Statutes at Large* 908, Ch. 406.

[12] See Senator Royal S. Copeland, "Defensive Alliances." *State Government,* 7:106, May, 1934.

[13] Joseph H. Hagan, "Crime Compact." *The Book of the States, 1948-49,* 7:50.

[14] *State Government,* 24:244, October, 1951. See also "Probation and Parole Compact." *The Book of the States, 1952-53,* 9:39. In the latter, mention is made of an amendment to the original compact, in the process of adoption, which will permit "out-of-state incarceration" of a violator in the receiving State and thereby render possible elimination of expensive returns of violators whose remaining terms of imprisonment in the sending State are short.

[15] See table, *The Book of the States, 1948-49,* 7:52, listing States operating under these various arrangements. Additions to the lists of signatory States in the period since compilation of the table indicated may be found in *State Government,* 24: 203, August, 1951, or in "New Ratifications or Amendments to Existing Interstate Compacts—1950-1951." *The Book of the States, 1952-53,* 9:23-24.

[16] Hagan, *loc. cit.* [17] See *supra,* Ch. IV.

[18] Frankfurter and Landis, *op. cit.,* p. 699.

[19] National Resources Committee, *op. cit.,* p. 38.

[20] See *Interstate Compacts in the Field of Labor Legislation; Report of the New Hampshire Commission on Interstate Compacts Affecting Labor and Industries* (Concord, N. H., 1935) and T. Bress, "Some Aspects of the Concord Interstate Compact on Labor." *St. John's Law Review,* 10:93-103, December, 1935.

[21] See Max Hall, "Child Labor Amendment Dead But Main Aims Are Now Laws," *Richmond Times-Dispatch,* April 24, 1949.

[22] See *Interstate Compacts in the Field of Labor Legislation,* p. 35. Clause taken from Title I of Compact.

[23] Townsend, *op. cit.,* pp. 87-88. [24] *Ibid.,* p. 87.

[18] Frankfurter and Landis, *op. cit.,* p. 699.

[26] "Interstate Compacts." *United States Law Review,* 70:565, October, 1936.

[27] "Industrial and Labor Ajustments [*sic*] by Interstate Compacts." *Marquette Law Review,* 20:19, December, 1935.

[28] Governor Tuck of Virginia said that he saw no chance whatever of such approval. See editorial, "An Issue Not of Sovereignty But of Common Sense," *Richmond Times-Dispatch,* April 9, 1949.

[29] *Ibid.* [30] *Ibid.*

[31] See opposing letter of John E. Mayo, Secretary of the Potomac River Oystermen's Association, in *Richmond Times-Dispatch,* April 4, 1949; letter of C. O'Connor Goolrick, Chairman of the Chesapeake Potomac Commission, in *Rich-*

mond Times-Dispatch, April 9, 1949, taking issue with "Oystermen's Spokesman"; letter of William S. Snow, former member of the State Commission of Game and Inland Fisheries, together with editorial entitled "Scope of the Proposed Bay Authority," commenting thereon, in *Richmond Times-Dispatch,* January 28, 1948; and editorials "Inaction Invites Intervention," *Richmond Times-Dispatch,* August 27, 1948, "Maryland-Virginia Peace Pact to Protect an Industry," *Richmond Times-Dispatch,* March 17, 1949, and "An Issue Not of Sovereignty But of Common Sense," *Richmond Times-Dispatch,* April 9, 1949. All has not been smooth in the relations of the two States in connection with these boundary waters and the marine resources which they contain. See July issues of *Richmond Times-Dispatch* for an indication of a flare-up in 1926. "Crab Trouble Ugly, Captain Wires Houston," *Richmond Times-Dispatch,* July 25, 1926; "Crabbing War Not Yet Over It Is Feared," *Richmond Times-Dispatch,* July 26, 1926. The Virginia-Maryland "Oysterman's War" flared anew when, on July 5, 1949, a Maryland crabber was slain by a Virginia officer. Developments can be traced in the *Baltimore Sun* and the *Richmond Times-Dispatch.* See "Shorewaterman Killed by New Inspector from Virginia Patrol Plane," *Baltimore Sun,* July 6, 1949; "Governor Lane's Responsibility," *Baltimore Sun,* July 7, 1949; "Virginia Deputy Jailed after Being Released on Bail in Murder Charge," *Baltimore Sun,* July 8, 1949; "Jurisdictional Dispute Seen," *Baltimore Sun,* July 8, 1949; "Maryland and Virginia Urged to End Bay, Potomac Dispute," *Baltimore Sun,* July 11, 1949; "Virginia Set a Hearing Aug. 5 in Bay Killing," *Baltimore Sun,* July 23, 1949; "Maryland Crabber Slain in Scuffle over Rifle with Virginia Officer," *Richmond Times-Dispatch,* July 6, 1949; "Maryland, Virginia Issue Warrant for Murder against Fisheries Deputy," *Richmond Times-Dispatch,* July 7, 1949; "Acree Jailed Twice in Case of Bay Slaying," *Richmond Times-Dispatch,* July 8, 1949; "Gunplay on Chesapeake Bay," *Richmond Times-Dispatch,* July 8, 1949; "Survey to Set Jurisdiction in Bay Slaying," *Richmond Times-Dispatch,* July 9, 1949; "Tuck, Lankford in Unannounced Parley Here Discuss Shooting of Marylander," *Richmond Times-Dispatch,* July 13, 1949; "Lane to Ask Extradition of Acree to Face Trial in Maryland for Slaying," *Richmond Times-Dispatch,* July 16, 1949; "Maryland-Virginia Division of Bay at Issue Again," *Richmond Times-Dispatch,* July 17, 1949; "Tuck Receives Maryland Call for Acree," *Richmond Times-Dispatch,* July 23, 1949.

[32] "Compact of 1785 May Head for Supreme Court Test," *Richmond Times-Dispatch,* February 13, 1951. The *Times-Dispatch* editorial writer notes that congressional consent has been presumed not to be required for the instant compact which antedates the United States Constitution. But, he observes, "While 'implied' consent of Congress has been taken for granted, the specific question, as it affects fisheries rights or regulations, has never passed a clear-cut test in the courts. The courts have held, however, that a State acting alone cannot abrogate a congressionally approved compact with another State. A test of the compact on constitutional grounds would seem to be Maryland's only hope for terminating a deal which has turned out to be of advantage only to Virginia. Commenting on this point a research report published by the Maryland Legislative Council in 1946 stated that: 'For one thing, a number of cases on the point (renunciation of an interstate compact by one State) have concerned vested and individual interests in lands or the use of waters. Since it could hardly be said that *any individual citizen* of Virginia has a vested interest in the continued use of the Potomac River, the reasons for upholding the Compact of 1785 might be correspondingly less convincing.'" *Cf.* treatment of the case of *Wharton* v. *Wise, supra,*

Ch. II, which deals with the validity of the 1785 compact.

[33] *The Book of the States, 1943-44,* 5:51.

[34] "The Atlantic States Marine Fisheries Commission." *The Book of the States, 1948-49,* 7:46.

[34a] *The Book of the States, 1952-53,* 9:23. See also Wayne D. Heydecker, "The Atlantic States Marine Fisheries Commission." *The Book of the States, 1952-53,* 9:31-32.

[35] See *The Book of the States, 1948-49,* 7:27, 43-44, and *ibid., 1950-51,* 8:42-44. The Pacific States Marine Fisheries Compact was ratified in 1947 by the States of California, Oregon, and Washington and granted the consent of Congress in the same year. The Gulf States Marine Fisheries Compact was ratified by the States of Alabama and Florida in 1947, Louisiana in 1948, Texas in 1949, and granted the consent of Congress in 1949.

[36] National Resources Committee, *op. cit.,* p. 43.

[37] These States produce more than 90 per cent of the nation's gas and 80 per cent of its crude oil. For a list of States signatory to the compact with ratification years see *The Book of the States, 1950-51,* 8:26.

[38] Arthur S. Davenport, "The Interstate Oil Compact Commission." *The Book of the States, 1948-49,* 7:41.

[39] National Resources Committee, *op. cit.,* p. 44.

[40] W. Brooke Graves, *American State Government* (3rd edition; Boston: D. C. Heath and Company, 1946), p. 908.

[41] 36 United States *Statutes at Large* 961, Ch. 186.

[42] "Is Federal Law Necessary to Avert Timber Famine?" *Richmond Times-Dispatch,* May 16, 1949.

[43] 63 United States *Statutes at Large* 271, Ch. 246.

[44] *The Book of the States, 1950-51,* 8:25; *ibid., 1952-53,* 9:23; Perry H. Merrill, "Northeastern Forest Fire Protection Commission." *The Book of the States, 1952-53,* 9:35-36.

[45] 63 United States *Statutes at Large* 272.

[46] *The Book of the States, 1950-51,* 8:25. [47] Article I.

[48] 49 United States *Statutes at Large* 1570, Ch. 688. [49] *Ibid.,* p. 1571.

[50] See Public Administration Clearing House *News Bulletin,* Release No. 2, Tuesday, February 1, 1949, and *The Book of the States, 1952-53,* 9:24.

[51] A well-known example of attempted solution of the equitable distribution problem by compact is the Colorado River Compact. See Reuel L. Olson, *The Colorado River Compact* (Los Angeles: The Author, 1926); National Resources Committee, *op. cit.,* Ch. VII; and *The Colorado River*: Interim Report on the Status of the Investigations Authorized to be Made by the Boulder Canyon Project Act and the Boulder Canyon Project Adjustment Act, House Document 419, 80th Congress, 1st session (Washington: Government Printing Office, 1947). See also John G. Will, "Upper Colorado River Commission." *The Book of the States, 1952-53,* 9:30-31.

[52] *New Jersey* v. *New York,* 283 U.S. 336, 342 (1931).

[53] The litigation method of solving the distribution problem proved unsatisfactory in the instant case. Incodel (the Interstate Commission on the Delaware River Basin) suggested that the interested States cease their attempts to achieve equitable distribution by means of costly litigation—it was estimated that approximately $1,000,000.00 had been expended by the several governments in that litigation — and strive for apportionment by agreement. The States reconciled

their differences and enacted identical and reciprocal legislation to govern the sharing of the Delaware water supply. See David W. Robinson, "The Interstate Commission on the Delaware River Basin." *The Book of the States, 1941-42,* 4:213 ff; also "The Interstate Commission on the Delaware River Basin." *The Book of the States, 1943-44,* 5:57-61; James H. Allen, "The Interstate Commission on the Delaware River Basin." *The Book of the States, 1945-46,* 6:30-32; James H. Allen, "Interstate Commission on the Delaware River Basin." *The Book of the States, 1948-49,* 7:35-37; James H. Allen, "The Interstate Commission on the Delaware River Basin." *The Book of the States, 1950-51,* 8:32-33; and *ibid., 1952-53,* 9:25.

[53a] For treatments of activities in this field see the articles on the various interstate sanitation commissions in *The Book of the States, 1952-53,* 9:25-30; James H. Allen, "The Interstate Commission on the Delaware River Basin," p. 25; Edwin R. Cotton, "Interstate Commission on the Potomac River Basin," p. 26; Edward J. Cleary, "Ohio River Valley Sanitation Commission," pp.27-28; Seth G. Hess, "Interstate Sanitation Commission," pp. 28-29; and Joseph G. Knox, "New England Interstate Water Pollution Control Commission," pp. 29-30.

[54] National Resources Committee, *op. cit.,* p. 43.

[55] 256 U.S. 296, 313 (1921).

[56] "Why An Ohio River Pollution Pact," *Richmond Times-Dispatch,* January 24, 1948. Some indication of the difficulties to be encountered by the individual State in enforcement of its anti-pollution program can be gleaned from an editorial, "Petersburg and Pollution," *Richmond Times-Dispatch,* May 18, 1949.

[57] An agency created by compact for the primary purpose of controlling and abating pollution in the Potomac River Basin.

[58] Edwin R. Cotton, "The Interstate Commission on the Potomac River Basin." *The Book of the States, 1948-49,* 7:37.

[59] James H. Allen, "The Interstate Commission on the Delaware River Basin," *The Book of the States, 1948-49,* 7:35-36.

[60] Frankfurter and Landis, *op. cit.,* p. 704.

[61] 42 United States *Statutes at Large* 1058, Ch. 431.

[62] Townsend, *op. cit.,* p. 88.

[63] The Virginia-Maryland agreement concerning the Potomac River affords an example, as does that of 1788 between Georgia and South Carolina dealing with the boundary between those States and the navigation of the Savannah River. The latter compact was held in *South Carolina* v. *Georgia,* 3 Otto (93 U.S.) 4 (1876), to be subject to the congressional commerce power, both States having adopted the Constitution subsequent to ratification of the agreement.

[64] National Resources Committee, *op. cit.,* p. 40.

[65] Frankfurter and Landis, *op. cit.,* p. 697.

[66] *Ibid.* [67] Article VI. [68] Article XI.

[69] "Port of New York Authority." *Fortune,* September, 1933, p. 22.

[70] National Resources Committee, *op. cit.,* p. 40.

[71] See *ibid.,* p. 41. See also C. Herman Pritchett, "The Paradox of the Government Corporation." *Public Administration Review,* 1:381, Summer, 1941, for a consideration of the government corporation. Professor Pritchett concludes that there is none of the "special 'corporate' characteristics which could not be given in the same way to a nonincorporated agency." *Ibid.,* p. 389.

[72] National Resources Committee, *op. cit.,* p. 41.

[73] "Port of New York Authority." *Fortune,* September, 1933, p. 25. Dimock

and Benson state that the Authority "has largely failed in its main job because of lack of power to force conflicting interests of interstate and foreign commerce into line – a weakness which is apparently inherent in the compact mode of government, where there is no use of federal power to support the states which are parties to the compact." Marshall E. Dimock and George C. S. Benson, *Can Interstate Compacts Succeed?* Public Policy Pamphlet, No. 22 (Chicago: The University of Chicago Press, 1937), p. 10.

[74] "Port of New York Authority." *Fortune,* September, 1933, p. 30. See also Erwin W. Bard, *The Port of New York Authority.* Studies in History, Economics and Public Law, edited by the Faculty of Political Science of Columbia University, No. 468 (New York: Columbia University Press; London: P. S. King & Staples, Ltd., 1942) and Lee K. Jaffe, "Port of New York Authority." *The Book of the States, 1952-53,* 9:37.

[75] Article I.

[76] National Resources Committee, *op. cit.,* p. 61. Chapter VII of this work is entitled "Interstate Compacts – The Colorado River Example."

[76a] Milton M. Kinsey, "Bi-State Development Agency." *The Book of the States, 1952-53,* 9:38.

[77] Frankfurter and Landis, *op. cit.,* p. 703.

[78] The agreement embraced chartering a company for the construction of a canal linking the Ohio River with the tidewater of the Potomac River. The Virginia act, "or so much thereof as respects the canal and works to be constructed in the District of Columbia, and the States of Virginia and Maryland," was to become effective upon the assent of Congress and of the Maryland legislature, "and upon receiving the further assent of the Legislature of Pennsylvania," the whole of the act was to become effective. *Virginia Laws,* 1823-24, Ch. 38, p. 41; *Maryland Laws,* 1824, Ch. 79, p. 53; 4 United States *Statutes at Large* 101, 292, 602; *Pennsylvania Acts,* 1825-26, Ch. 7, p. 8, as amended by Act of March 9, 1826, *Pennsylvania Acts,* 1825-26, Ch. 28, p. 73. A list of these acts is published in 4 United States *Statutes at Large,* Appendix I.

[79] "Civil Defense in the States," *State Government,* 23:237-45, 257, November, 1950. This article summarizes the progress of each of the States in civil defense.

[80] Leonard Dreyfuss, "Interstate Civil Defense Cooperation," *State Government,* 23:246, November, 1950. For text of agreement and brief defining its terms see "New York-New Jersey Mutual Aid Agreement," *ibid.,* pp. 247, 257.

[81] *Ibid.,* p. 247.

[82] *State Government,* 24:202, August, 1951. See also F. L. Zimmermann and Mitchell Wendell, "Interstate Compacts." *The Book of the States, 1952-53,* 9:20-23, for the section dealing with Civil Defense. The authors also appended "A Note on Civil Defense" to their study, *The Interstate Compact since 1925* (Chicago: The Council of State Governments, 1951), p. 127.

[83] *State Government,* 24:45, March, 1951. [84] *Ibid.*

[85] *Missouri ex. rel. Gaines* v. *Canada,* 305 U.S. 337 (1938).

[86] 163 U.S. 537 (1896). In this case the Court sustained a Louisiana statute requiring railroads to provide equal but separate accommodations for the white and colored races as not in violation of the "equal protection" clause of the Fourteenth Amendment.

[87] *Missouri ex rel. Gaines* v. *Canada,* 306 U.S. 337, 349 (1938).

[88] *Ibid.,* p. 350.

[89] *Ibid.,* p. 351. In a per curiam decision handed down in *Sipuel* v. *Board of*

Regents of the University of Oklahoma, 332 U.S. 631 (1948), the Court held Sipuel, a Negro concededly qualified to receive the professional legal education offered by the State, to be entitled to secure legal education "afforded *by a state institution.*" (Italics mine). The Court relied on its decision in the *Gaines* case.

According to a news-item, "Negro Woman Is Enrolled to Study Law in Oklahoma," *Richmond Times-Dispatch,* June 19, 1949, Mrs. Ada Lois (Sipuel) Fisher on June 18 "completed her enrollment in the University of Oklahoma law school — 41 months after she first sought admission." To comply with the ruling of the Court in the *Sipuel* case the State established a "makeshift law school" as a branch of Langston University, a state university maintained for Negroes. Sipuel and other Negroes shunned it, and it is being abandoned. Sipuel started a new court action to gain admission to the white university. In *Fisher* v. *Hurst,* 333 U.S. 147 (1948), barely a month after the *Sipuel* decision, she asked leave of the Supreme Court to file a petition for a writ of mandamus to compel compliance with the Court's mandate issued in the earlier case. The Court in a per curiam decision denied her motion, pointing out that the state district court had issued an order in accord with the Supreme Court ruling and had retained jurisdiction to hear and determine in the first instance any question arising under that order. Probably the Court was influenced in its decision by the short lapse of time between the *Sipuel* case and the motion in *Fisher* v. *Hurst.* The State passed a law permitting the enrollment of Negroes in the white university when the courses they sought were not offered at the Negro school. Twenty-nine Negroes have enrolled in the University of Oklahoma under the law. University officials say the Negroes will be "seated in special segregated parts of classrooms until sufficient extra personnel can be provided to set up separate Negro classes."

[90] *Nashville Banner,* October 20, 1947. *Cf.* Clyde L. Ball, "Constitutionality of the Proposed Regional Plan for Professional Education of the Southern Negro." *Vanderbilt Law Review,* 1:403, 405, footnote 11, April, 1948, and "Regional Education: A New Use of the Interstate Compact?" *Virginia Law Review,* 34:74, January, 1948.

[91] *Congressional Record,* Vol. 94, pt. 4, p. 5576, May 11, 1948.

[92] *Ibid.,* pt. 5, p. 5763, May 13, 1948. [93] *Ibid.,* pt. 4, p. 5270, May 4, 1948.

[94] On the 24th of February, 1948, in the House of Representatives, and on the 25th of February, in the Senate, there were introduced identical joint resolutions "giving the consent of Congress to the compact on regional education entered into between the Southern States at Tallahassee, Fla., on February 8, 1948." *Ibid.,* pt. 2, pp. 1658, 1660. Twenty-nine Senators from fifteen Southern States introduced the measure in the Senate. Senate Joint Resolution 191 giving the consent of Congress to the compact was approved by the Senate Committee on the Judiciary and placed on the calendar on April 13, 1948. *Ibid.,* pt. 4, p. 4368. On May 4, 1948, the House of Representatives passed the companion measure, House Joint Resolution 334. *Ibid.,* p. 5275. The House Joint Resolution granted consent to the compact among those States listed above "and such other States named therein (in the compact) who have or may become parties thereto, to wit, the States of Virginia, West Virginia, North Carolina, Kentucky, Louisiana, and Oklahoma." *Ibid.* The House action was reported to the Senate on May 5, 1948 (*ibid.,* p. 5283), and when Senate Joint Resolution 191 was laid before the Senate on May 6, House Joint Resolution 334 was substituted for it. *Ibid.,* p. 5411. The Senate after extended debate voted to refer this resolution to committee for further consideration. *Ibid.,* pt. 5, p. 5777, May 13, 1948. Consequently the reference of

House Joint Resolution 334 to the Senate Committe on the Judiciary was substantially the same thing as a recommital of Senate Joint Resolution 191 and amounted to "burial in committee" of the approving resolution.

[95] See editorial, "Better Education for Less in Dixie," *Richmond Times-Dispatch,* October 26, 1947, and "Regional Education: A New Use of the Interstate Compact?" *Virginia Law Review,* 34:74, January, 1948.

[96] "Better Education for Less in Dixie," *Richmond Times-Dispatch,* October 26, 1947.

[97] *Ibid.* Italics mine.

[98] "Regional Schools Approved," *Richmond Times-Dispatch,* April 13, 1948.

[99] See *Congressional Record,* May 6-13, 1948.

[100] *Ibid.,* Vol. 94, pt. 5, pp. 5659, 5661, May 12, 1948.

[101] "Wisdom from Utah on Civil Rights," *Atlanta Journal,* May 16, 1948.

[102] *Ibid.*

[103] See Note, "Segregation in Public Schools—A Violation of 'Equal Protection of the Laws'." *Yale Law Journal,* 56:1059, June, 1947, where it is contended that compulsory segregation necessarily implies social inferiority of the minority and constitutes, therefore, a denial of equal protection of the laws. The assumption that compulsory segregation does not imply social inferiority, basic to the decision in the *Plessy* case, "has become untenable in the light of our present knowledge of psychology and sociology." *Ibid.,* p. 1066. The writer argues that the *Plessy* case should be overruled.

[104] *Congressional Record,* Vol. 94, pt. 5, p. 5671, May 12, 1948. [105] *Ibid.*

[106] *Ibid.,* p. 5660. In this connection see treatment of *Virginia* v. *Tennessee, supra,* Chs. II and III.

[107] *Ibid.,* p. 5823, May 13, 1948.

[108] "Southern States Going Forward with Plan for Regional Schools," *Atlanta Journal,* August 3, 1948. *Cf.* "Regional Education Goes Forward," *Richmond Times-Dispatch,* August 6, 1948. See also Wright Bryan's editorial, "The South Has Made Progress Toward Fair Treatment of Races," *Atlanta Journal,* August 1, 1948, written initially for the *Baltimore Evening Sun,* July 26, 1948, as an expression of the Southern viewpoint regarding the civil rights controversy.

[109] Mr. Morse's contention was expressed in his statement: "I want to say to the Senators from Virginia, West Virginia, Vermont, and New Hampshire that those four States already give us two gaad precedents fornot approving this compact. Those States have arrangements between themselves which have never been approved by Congress. In the case of Virginia and West Virginia their agreement is for the use of an educational institution at Richmond. In the case of Vermont and New Hampshire, I am told, it covers the joint use of a penitentiary. Those are precedents against the necessity of approval of this compact by this body. I say that there has never been presented in the debate a single precedent which justifies our taking jurisdiction over a subject matter such as is contained in the compact. In the interest of keeping State rights in education protected I say that this particular proposal should be referred to the committee for further consideration and study." *Congressional Record,* Vol. 94, pt. 5, p. 5777, May 13, 1948. Morse contended that congressional consent was unnecessary for this type of agreement but that, if it were to be given, it should be predicated upon an anti-segregation stipulation.

[110] Professor Edward S. Corwin thinks that the Supreme Court would sustain the legality of regional institutions for Negroes if such institutions were to be

established under an interstate compact approved by Congress. Professor Corwin says: "I base my opinion that a regional university for Negroes in the South would be constitutional on three considerations: 1. That what a state can do for itself it can—at least there is nothing to the contrary—do in association with other states by means of a compact to which Congress has given its consent. 2. In giving its consent to such a compact Congress would not only exercise its powers under Article I, Section 10, but also its powers under the 5th section of the 14th Amendment. 3. That the court, recognizing that the states could provide much better education in the manner suggested than they could individually, would certainly sustain such a compact." Virginius Dabney, *Below the Potomac; A Book About the New South* (New York & London: D. Appleton-Century Company, Incorporated, 1942), p. 222. According to Professor Corwin's view congressional consent would constitute an exercise of its "power to enforce, by appropriate legislation," the provisions of the Fourteenth Amendment. Whether he would think the Court apt to sustain the regional education pact in the face of Congress' failure to grant its consent would probably depend on the weight which he would ascribe to his third consideration. See *supra*, Ch. II, for treatment of *Virginia* v. *Tennessee* dictum as to whether some compacts may not be valid without congressional consent. This dictum was the basis for the contention of many Senators that consent for the regional pact was unnecessary. This contention, though clearly motivated in part by political considerations, is of interest in connection with the problem raised by the *Virginia* v. *Tennessee* dictum. It was argued in the Senate that, education being so clearly within the reserved powers of the States, a compact on that subject did not require congressional consent. If this implies that consent is unnecessary whenever the agreement relates to a matter within the reserved powers of the States, the implication is questionable. Addressing the question, "Is Consent of Congress Necessary?" Millard Caldwell summarizes the negative case. He covers the *Virginia* v. *Tennessee* dictum and points to the Court's reliance upon it in the case of *Wharton* v. *Wise*. He continues: "In 1935 a Federal judge (14 Fed. Suppl. 596) set forth the principle that Congress should be called upon to ratify agreements only on such matters 'as affected the national supremacy and such matters only.' State courts have generally followed this rule, and as recently as 1939 the petition for certiorari in *Dixie Wholesale Grocery* v. *Martin* (308 U.S. 609), a Kentucky case, was denied, and the Supreme Court thereby gave its tacit approval to the old ruling in *Virginia* v. *Tennessee*. Whether the consent of Congress to the compact is necessary is not a pressing question. The Southern States made application to Congress for approval of the compact, but Congress has not acted. The chief opponents of the plan insist that the consent of Congress is not necessary. Education is already generally accepted as a responsibility of the State, rather than of the Federal Government. Therefore, it is difficult to see how the regional compact could be construed to 'increase the political power of the States in such a manner as to encroach upon, weaken or interfere with the just supremacy of the United States.'" "Legal Aspects of the Regional Plan for Higher Education," *Higher Education*, 6:104, January 1, 1950.

[111] "Regional Education: A New Use of the Interstate Compact?" *Virginia Law Review*, 34:74, footnote 66, January, 1948. An editorial from the *New York Times* advances the basis for NAACP opposition: "The regional college solution of the South's Negro educational problem has encountered the formidable opposition of the National Association for the Advancement of Colored People on the ground that it continues the principle of segregation, and that therefore inequali-

ties are 'inevitable'." "A Regional College Plan," *New York Times,* January 1, 1949. The NAACP would seem to be opposing the law as it stands in this matter, for according to the *Plessy* v. *Ferguson* rule segregation is permissable if accomodations or facilities are equal. See *supra,* Ch. V.

The NAACP sent to every Congressman a letter in which it stated: "Our principal reasons for opposing this resolution [approval for the Southern States Regional Education Compact] are these: 1. The testimony of the proponents of this legislation before the subcommittee of the Senate Judiciary Committee established by their own admission that the regional institutions would be operated on a segregated basis. It is also an undisputed fact that the laws of every State signatory to this compact require segregation in education. 2. It is our conviction after careful consideration of all the facts and surrounding circumstances, that it represents a bold attempt to circumvent decisions of the Supreme Court of the United States . . . which require States to furnish to Negro students educational opportunity equal to that furnished white students within the State boundaries. 3. Congress should not put its stamp of approval on racial segregation." *Congressional Record,* Vol. 94, pt. 4, p. 5271, May 4, 1948. Reason number 2 constitutes the main legal point at issue and poses the principal hurdle which the Southern States will probably have to face in any test case of the compact's validity.

The Negro newspaper, Norfolk-Portsmouth *Journal and Guide,* in an editorial of November 1, 1947, entitled "The South's Regional Graduate School Proposal," expresses the view that "the five reasons given by C. A. Scott, editor and general manager of the *Atlanta Daily World,* form the logical basis of the oposition [*sic*]. Editor Scott said: '(1) It would be discriminatory; (2) it would be a sort of monstrosity that would be everybody's business and in the end nobody's business; (3) the proposed university would be inferior to the average southern white graduate and professional school; (4) the regional school would be less advantageous to colored students than the scholarship program, and (5) it does not meet the requirements of the United States Supreme Court decision in the Gaines case'." The editor of the Norfolk-Portsmouth *Journal and Guide* poses the question: "Is this proposal [for the establishment of advanced regional schools in the South] indicative of a sincere and conscientious effort on the part of the governors to broaden the educational opportunities for the Negro in the South, or merely a studied effort to circumvent the mandate of the United States Supreme Court in the Gaines case?" His own view of the regional school program is indicated in his observation that "admittedly, it requires a broader faith than most of us possess to look with hope upon a Negro educational center deriving its support from a combination of a half dozen or more southern states, with many of their legislatures filled with reactionaries of the most bourbon type. . . . The idea may be proposed to Negro Americans as an educational bonanza, but it inspires no jubilation on their part." This editorial has been termed a reflection of the "view of the Negro press." See "Regional Education: A New Use of the Interstate Compact?" *Virginia Law Review,* 34:74, footnote 66, January, 1948.

[112] "Regional Education: A New Use of the Interstate Compact?" *Virginia Law Review,* 34:75-76, January, 1948.

[113] For text of compact see *Congressional Record,* Vol. 94, pt. 4, pp. 5270-71, May 4, 1948.

[114] It has been suggested that the wording of the Court in the *Gaines* case might not have been the same had regional schools been on the horizon at the time. "True, the Court suggests that these requirements [of equal facilities]

can only be met by an institution which is located within the borders of the state, but the particular wording is not essential to the holding in the case, and there is no indication that the Court has considered the possibility of a regional school being established. What the Court actually held in the *Gaines* case was that it was not sufficient for the State to pay tuition in an out-of-state institution over which the State had no control, and to which the State had no duty to contribute. The *Sipuel* case held that equal facilities must be furnished in a state institution." Clyde L. Ball, "Constitutionality of the Proposed Regional Plan for Professional Education of the Southern Negro." *Vanderbilt Law Review,* 1:416, April, 1948. It might be noted that colored opponents to the regional plan point out that the *Gaines* case prompted serious consideration of the regional school compact. But there is a difference between evasion and avoidance of a Supreme Court ruling.

[115] "Regional Education: A New Use of the Interstate Compact?" *Virginia Law Review,* 34:76, January, 1948. Another legal analyst observes that "the Court has tended to consider factual results rather than technical and sometimes meaningless legal considerations in reaching its decisions. . . . It [the project] represents a real advance over existing opportunities for the Negro. . . . The Court, then, may let nice questions of theoretical equality yield to the concrete facts of substantially equal opportunity as established by the regional plan." Ball, *op. cit.,* p. 419.

[116] "Legal Hurdles to Regionalism," *Richmond Times-Dispatch,* December 16, 1948.

[117] "A Regional College Plan," *New York Times,* January 1, 1949.

[118] Ball, *op. cit.,* p. 418.

[119] Millard Caldwell, "Legal Aspects of the Regional Plan for Higher Education." *Higher Education,* 6:105, January 1, 1950.

[119a] Board of Control for Southern Regional Education, *The South's Regional Education Program, A Progress Report* (Atlanta, Ga., November, 1951), p. 6. See *McCready* v. *Byrd,* 73 A. 2d 8 (1950) and *Byrd* v. *McCready,* 340 U.S. 827 (1950).

[120] See John E. Ivey, Jr., "The Southern Regional Education Program." *The Book of the States, 1952-53,* 9:263-64.

[120a] "The Regional Idea Grows," *Richmond Times-Dispatch,* October 18, 1949 (editorial).

[121] "South Begins Co-operative School Plan," *Richmond Times-Dispatch,* June 12, 1949 (news-item).

[122] "Regional Education Plans: A Far-Reaching Southern Step," *Richmond Times- Dispatch,* May 25, 1949. This editorial would seem to indicate settlement of a question which existed earlier as to Virginia's ability to participate. A *Richmond Times-Dispatch* editorial of December 16, 1948, entitled "Legal Hurdles to Regionalism," pointed to a "legal hurdle" which might have to be cleared before Virginia could participate in the projected plan. "This is to be found in Section 141 of the State Constitution, which provides that 'no appropriation of public funds shall be made to any school or institution of learning not owned or exclusively controlled by the State or some political subdivision thereof.' Since funds are now being appropriated from the State Treasury to Meharry Medical College at Nashville, for Virginia Negroes to study medicine and dentistry there, it is possible that this constitutional section does not block the more ambitious regional plan. Official interpretation of the law is being awaited."

[123] John E. Ivey, Jr., and William J. McGlothlin, "The South's Evolving Pattern

of Regional Planning in Higher Education." *Higher Education,* 6:101, January 1, 1950.

[124] Board of Control for Southern Regional Education, *op. cit.,* p. 4. *Cf.* "Regional Study Plan Is Growing," *Tallahassee Democrat,* January 15, 1952 (editorial).

[125] "South Begins Co-operative School Plan," *Richmond Times-Dispatch,* June 12, 1949 (news item).

[126] Ivey and McGlothlin, *op. cit.,* p. 100.

[127] "Regional Education in the South: Three Governors Speak," *State Government,* 23:266, December, 1950.

[128] *State Government,* 24:12, January, 1951.

[129] The Western Governors' Conference consists of the Governors of eleven States and two Territories: Alaska, Arizona, California, Colorado, Hawaii, Idaho, Montana, Nevada, New Mexico, Oregon, Utah, Washington, and Wyoming.

[130] This account is based upon O. Meredith Wilson's article "The Western States and Territories Plan for Regional Education." *Higher Education,* 7:197-8, May 1, 1951. For a treatment of activities more restricted in scope within the same area see G. D. Humphrey's article, "Regional Planning in Higher Education for the Rocky Mountain States." *Higher Education,* 6:107-9, January 1, 1950. Humphrey, President of the University of Wyoming, points out that the "success of the cooperative arrangements with respect to the river basins in the Rocky Mountain States, together with the fact that this region does not have such barriers to overcome as race segregation, low per capita wealth, and others which must be contended with in some other sections of the country, will mean that the program of regional higher education in the Rocky Mountain States, once under way, will proceed more rapidly than it might under different circumstances." *Ibid.,* p. 109.

[131] *State Government,* 24:145, June, 1951.

[132] Alice Mary Dodd, "Interstate Compacts." *United States Law Review,* 70:573, October, 1936.

[133] "Progress and Prospects in the States." *State Government,* 24:12, January, 1951.

[134] Dodd, *op. cit.,* p. 572. New Hampshire law authorizes the trustees of the state prison "to contract with the authorities of other states having penal institutions in which female convicts are kept separate or apart from male convicts, for the care, custody, maintenance, and confinement in such institutions of females convicted under the laws of this state of offenses punishable by imprisonment in the state prison." Such contracts are subject to approval by the Governor and council. New Hampshire law with respect to diminution of the length of sentence for good behavior or other cause is applicable to "all sentences served in whole or in part in such out-of-state institutions." *Revised Laws of New Hampshire, 1942,* Ch. 464. The law prescribes the New Hampshire system relative only to the care and custody of female convicts. The New Hampshire State Prison provides for the male convicts. Letter from Enoch D. Fuller, Secretary of State, State of New Hampshire, June 15, 1949.

[135] See "Mental Health." *State Government,* 23:183, August, 1950; "Progress and Prospects in the States." *State Government,* 24:12, January, 1951.

Chapter VI

UTILITY AND LIMITATIONS OF THE COMPACT DEVICE

The compact device has both staunch advocates and staunch opponents. The device has been criticized for its inflexibility, for its slowness in negotiation and amendment, for its reliance upon "equal" States as components rather than upon "real" regions, for its requirement of unanimity among the States to which it is applicable, for its tendency to realize a "lowest common denominator" in the prescription of standards, and for its inadequacy for, or inapplicability to, fields of continuing functions and fields of conflicting interests. Thus the compact has been termed a "clumsy and futile substitute for effective national action."[1]

Some of these same criticisms are praise for the device to some of its supporters. The very fact that it does rely upon the States as component units is gratifying to states' rights advocates. Moreover, the prescription of some standard, even though it be the "lowest common denominator," is preferable to no standard in fields where States cannot act individually without injury to themselves. The "lowest common denominator" might itself be termed a misnomer, the "most *common* denominator" being preferable. Some look to its use as a means of conciliating popular demand for action in the sphere of social legislation and at the same time avoiding concomitant enlargement of central government.[2] Others support its use as a device permitting the solution of social problems not susceptible to unilateral attack by a State and maintaining unimpaired the validity of the State as what Mr. Justice Brandeis once termed a "laboratory" in which "novel social and economic experiments" may be tried by its citizens "without risk to the rest of the country."[3]

As Professor Macmahon puts it, the compact device has been "extolled as a method of dealing with problems beyond the limited powers of the nation and the incongruous limits of the states." It has been urged "not merely as an expedient but as a desirable substitute for national action."[4] In an editorial which comments on the Twentieth Century acceleration in the rate of recourse to the compact device and the increase in the number of uses to which it is put, the "development among the States toward voluntary, co-operative effort" is termed encouraging. Interstate agreements, "if conscientiously fulfilled, furnish an excellent means of dealing with regional problems in a manner compatible with the principles of States' rights."[5]

The element of "conscientious fulfillment" upon which the editorialist's adjective "excellent" hinges depends to a great extent upon motivation. The matter of enforcement is of concern in this connection. The problem is what can be done about the State which defaults in its compact obligation. Other States which are parties to the compact can seek a court decree compelling the State which defaults to meet its obligation.[6] The specter of the *Virginia* v. *West Virginia*[7] series arises immediately as a reminder of the difficulties inherent in this method of securing compliance. Yet the Supreme Court asserted there its power to enforce its decree against a "sovereign" State, and its failure to indicate the specific means by which enforcement would be achieved is of little import. It has been said, probably quite correctly, that "In practice . . . there has not been a case on record in which a state of the Union has steadfastly refused to obey the decision of the Supreme Court in an interstate suit. It seems unlikely, in view of this history, that a lack of sanctions will render legal remedies against delinquent states inefficacious. Besides, the Supreme Court has said that when Congress has given its consent to a compact, it is likewise given power to enforce it. The evidence of experience seems to justify the conclusion that the 'unenforceability of compacts' argument has been overemphasized, and that, in reality, the success or failure of a compact depends only to a very minor degree upon whether it can be legally enforced."[8]

It cannot be said, of course, that effectiveness can be insured always by a judicial decree to enforce compliance. Effectiveness depends often upon the spirit of compliance, the character of administration, and, for that matter, upon participation of all the States necessary for the success of the compact. It is entirely possible, as has been pointed out, that States "may, because of their sovereign characteristics, avoid carrying-out the agreement, chiefly by enacting legislation that cunningly violates the spirit of the compact without perceptibly affecting the letter."[9] Moreover, the enthusiasm with which officials administer laws adopted to effectuate an agreement might indeed wane with elections and consequent changes in the personnel of the government. Professor Macmahon points out that "On the administrative even more than on the judicial side compacts are likely to draw strength from national infusions."[10] The Federal Government's use of its power over interstate commerce to block shipment from a State of oil produced in violation of the state law illustrates the way in which cooperative action on the part of the general and the state governments can ease the administrative problem of the State.[11] Rigid enforcement within the State of the regulations adopted in pursuance of the compact may be rendered easier, or even possible, by such federal legislation. It may be argued, however, that where federal action is essential to make the state action effective, the program might better be undertaken wholly on a federal level.

Enough has been said earlier to indicate that compacts with respect to such things as minimum labor standards or regulation of industry, for example, must be either widespread or coincident with the problem area, if they are to succeed. The reasons are obvious. Yet, it is equally obvious that it may be to the advantage of a given State to refrain from adherence to a compact as a means of attracting industry or of gaining a competitive advantage. Professor Joseph J. Spengler points out that the use of interstate compacts to solve economic problems is limited by the very nature of economic processes and interrelationships. He asserts that "In virtually every, if not in every, instance in which an important economic control by means of an interstate compact is or may be proposed, the compact will result in economic injury to the non-compacting states, or failure of the non-compacting states to establish controls similar to those established within the compacting states will result in injury to the compacting states."[12] Professor Spengler argues that the "high degree of integration of economic life to which such boundary-transcending effects and injuries are traceable, combined with the necessity that policy be determined by and class conflict resolved within a body representative of all interests, renders national legislative control superior to either state control or regional control by means of interstate compacts."[13]

The examples considered are fields where real conflict of interest may exist. Professors Dimock and Benson observe that, in general, "matters on the administrative level (i. e., those that can be dealt with rationally and objectively, involving little or no conflict of interest) are much more likely to be the subjects of successful interstate . . . agreements than are those on the political or emotional plane."[14] There is little concern over compliance or enforcement in connection with a compact related to such a matter as crime control. A State lives up to its agreement to permit "hot pursuit" because it wishes reciprocal permission from other States. Denial of the privileges of the compact is one possible "sanction" which influences each State to abide by its "bargain." Some similar consideration in all probability prompts the State initially to enter the agreement.

The compact negotiation is a slow and cumbersome process at best. Miss Dodd considers the length of time required to consummate a compact one of the largest drawbacks to use of the device. The formal equality of the States complicates negotiation and renders it somewhat comparable to international negotiation.[15] George Soule points to the difficulty inherent in negotiating a compact and brands the compact as " a clumsy attempt to duplicate the Federal government itself, when the Federal government is prevented from acting. The States originally got together and formed a national government to serve their common needs. Now they are obliged to come together again and make treaties with one another, instead of having the legislature of their Federal government pass the desired laws. The negotiation of a treaty is a delicate and difficult matter. It has to be ratified by the separate legislatures. In order to be effective, it requires the unanimous consent of the States involved; whereas in legislatures a majority is sufficient. No government ever worked well by unanimous consent. . . . . . . the interstate compact is even more clumsy and difficult than a Constitutional amendment, which can be ratified by three-quarters of the States. If the people of this country must rely on separate Constitutional amendments for every addition to important economic legislation, we are sunk. To rely on interstate compacts is even more hopeless than that."[16]

Professor Laski vividly presents a pessimistic view of the effect of time considerations on the utility of the compact device:

"No doubt . . . the Compact Clause of the Constitution offers the necessary possibilities of transcending state limits; but any careful survey of its achievements, even when it is undertaken . . . with goodwill towards, and faith in, its opportunities, suggests that the Compact Clause requires something like geological time to achieve the results that are desirable. But the United States, with all its resources, has not geological time at its disposal. On the contrary, the evidence is both abundant and growing that it must seek to make area coincide with function if it is at once to avoid excessive centralization and to be in a position effectively to deal with the social and economic issues before it. . . . Yet few observers of the American scene would regard a centralized United States as likely to be both efficient and free."[17]

It may be that the Colorado River Compact arrangement providing that the compact should become operative when ratified by the legislatures of six of the seven negotiating States affords a means of mitigating the evil of "slowdown." At least the arrangement prevents a single State from blocking action as one State might under a unanimity requirement. On the other hand, the refusal of one State to participate may defeat either the making or the effectiveness of some compacts. Yet the inordinate length of time which is required to consummate an interstate compact must be considered when the device is weighed against other forms of interstate cooperative action or federal action to achieve a desired goal.

Another criticism has been that the compact is too inflexible to be of more than limited utility.[18] Particularly, it has been urged that the inflexibility of the device renders its worth questionable in the fields of "social legislation." It is true that a compact may be modified by a procedure similar to that of its original negotiation, but such a modification might well prove as difficult of attainment as the compact's negotiation. Moreover, the compact may unduly curtail the state legislature's range in the enactment of statutory provisions relative to the problem. Arrangements have been devised which meet in part the criticisms directed at the inflexibility of the compact device. Some compacts make provisions for a revision date or a termination date. Either lessens the possibility of ossification and permits assessment of experience.[19] The danger that a compact prescribing standards will result in lowering of standards in some of the more progressive participating States may be offset somewhat by a provision that nothing in the compact is to be construed as interfering with retention or enactment of laws establishing higher standards than those set by the compact.

The element of rigidity in the device must be studied in the light of the use to which the compact is to be put. The very characteristics which render it ill-adapted to serve certain purposes are distinct advantages for other purposes. Dimock and Benson note claims, for example, that "rigidity is desirable, if not absolutely indispensable, in such fields as commerical law, uniform statutes, interstate crime-law enforcement, tax reform, and perhaps labor law."[20] Certainly compacts for the settlement of boundary disputes aim at finality. Moreover the contractual character of the device has proved of undoubted advantage in connection with interstate arrangements for such things as the construction of a bridge across an interestate river.[21] The device, then, may be considered well-adapted to the solution of a problem or dispute which can be setttled "once and for all." Dimock and Benson observe further, however, that any administrative venture for the solution of a problem or dispute which cannot be settled "once and for all" is "almost sure" to be unbusinesslike "without a certain allowance for discretion and alteration of detail, . . . for it will lack independence, initiative, and coercive authority."[22]

The Technical Committee on Regional Planning of the National Resources Committee urges, quite correctly it would seem, that the use of the compact device should be confined to appropriate subject matter.[23] It points out that the compact has proved unsatisfactory as a medium for continuous and progressive planning activity. This ineptitude is largely because of insufficiency in the grant of power to the compact agency independently to formulate and execute its plans. Hence, the agency must be forever seeking additional grants of authority and approval for its actions. This failing is difficult to eliminate from the compact device. For "sovereign States" combine in whatever venture is projected in the compact, and "sovereign States" are loath to relinquish sufficient authority to permit an interstate agency to formulate and execute plans free of control by the States in the combination. Yet, a compact stipulating the precise measures to be taken by the agency acts as a strait-jacket precluding the agency's effective operation as a planning and development body. Legislatures are not omniscient and hence cannot foresee all the contingencies which may develop to plague the agency.

Dimock and Benson observe, too, that the experience of the Colorado River Compact and the Port of New York Authority "augurs little good for the interstate compact as a means of settling serious conflicts of interests between states."[24] With respect to the Colorado River Compact the States of Arizona and California were unable to agree on the apportionment of waters among the lower basin States. It is questionable, however, whether any other method would prove more successful in producing agreement over so important an issue as the apportionment of a limited supply of life-giving water. The National Resources Committee concludes that the compact device is a suitable instrument for the solution of governmental problems or controversies which can be settled 'once and for all," such as boundary disputes, for the solution of issues involving only two States, and for the treatment of "subject matter involving definite conclusions and uniform laws to be administered through already existing departments of government."[25] From these conclusions the Committee deduces that the device should not be recommended for situations involving the opposite set of circumstances, "that is, when the problem is a continuing one; when the solution demands the establishment of independent machinery over and above the separate State departments; and when independent planning and autonomous execution are clearly indicated." Dimock and Benson state, on the other hand, that the "limitations on subject matter . . . seem to be matters of gradation and degree and subject to expansion with the passage of time."[26] They see a real future in the service of the compact device to the nation in view of the trend toward "objectivization of problems once considered 'unsuitable'" for compacts and in view of the possibility of aid from the Federal Government to strengthen the compact.[27] In spite of discouraging difficulties in its use, these writers think the compact idea should be utilized wherever it appears applicable.

The trend seems to be in a direction designed to test the accuracy of these conclusions as to the proper range of the compact. In recent years many compacts have created interstate commissions with continuing authority to plan, to make recommendations to the governments of the States of which they are the agents, and, in an increasing number of cases, even to make and enforce regulations. Moreover, these agreements are among considerable groups of States rather than restricted in each case to only two States. Examples are afforded by the Atlantic States Marine Fisheries Commission, the Gulf States Marine Fisheries Commission, the Pacific States Marine Fisheries Commission, the New England Interstate Water Pollution Control Commission, the Ohio River Valley Water Sanitation Commission, and the Interstate Commission on the Potomac River Basin.[28]

Some indication of other forms of interstate cooperative action, together with their weak and strong points, is essential to an evaluation of the strength and weakness of the compact device. Interstate cooperation can be achieved through the adoption of uniform laws (*i. e.*, textually identical statutes enacted by the individual States); or through the adoption of uniform administrative policies (*i. e.*, simple uniform or cooperative action by arrangements made on the administrative level, as through the various conferences of administrators); or through the development of uniform principles of judicial interpretation. Uniform judicial interpretation can be secured by having one State adopt verbatim the law of another State which has already been judicially construed. The National Conference of Commissioners on Uniform State Laws in drafting projects for laws for the consideration of the States has inserted clauses calling for uniformity of judicial interpretation of the laws.[29]

These types of interstate cooperation lie outside the ambit of the Compact Clause and do not require congressional consent. The resulting arrangement can be incorporated into a compact, however, to overcome some of the weaknesses of this type of cooperative action. Otherwise, there is no guarantee that the States will adhere to the arrangement for any given period; there may be serious disparity in enforcement from State to State; and there is no certainty of participation by the number of States necessary to effectiveness of the arrangement's provisions. These are weakness which probably would prove disastrous to cooperation in the controversial fields. On the other hand, these methods of achieving cooperative action between or among States may be devised much more rapidly, in that they are less formal and have less time-consuming negotiation requirements than the compact method. Moreover, they are not contractual in nature and, therefore, are probably less subject to the danger of "ossification." For some matters in non-controversial, technical fields where it is to everyone's advantage to have uniform legislation, as on uniform bills of lading for interstate shipment, the adoption of uniform laws provides an effective means of achieving the goal.[30] The weaknesses of the foregoing arrangements may be rectified, perhaps, by making such arrangements reciprocal, as for example, recognition by one State of the professional registrations of another contingent upon reciprocity. Compliance rests upon the desirability of the privilege granted and its denial to States failing to enact reciprocal legislation or to enforce its provisions once enacted. Whether this type arrangement does or does not require congressional consent is debatable.[31]

The compact device is the one method of interstate cooperative action which comes before a representative body of the nation for consideration in the light of broad public policy. The requirement of congressional consent affords Congress an opportunity to view the compact's projected treatment of regional problems with respect to its bearing on the welfare of the nation as a whole. The Supreme Court in indicating that some compacts did not require for their validity the consent of Congress was careful to stipulate that its words applied to those compacts which could in no way concern the United States and to cover under the consent requirement any combination tending to the increase of political power in the States which might encroach upon or interfere with the just supremacy of the United States.[32]

The compact device, then, has certain characteristics which render it well-adapted to serve some purposes and ill-adapted to serve others. It must, therefore, be studied in the light of the use to which it is to be put. It is not to be conceived as a substitute for national action. Alongside national action the compact will probably take its place with other elements as parts of what Professor Macmahon terms the "process which is crisscrossing all political boundaries with the lines of functional union."[33] This process and the preservation of the compact as one of its elements may well be, as Professor Laski suggests, essential to efficiency and to freedom. The compact as one of the elements in this process, moreover, may be essential to preservation of the vitality and potency of the States and to avoidance of an overladen general government.

[1] George Soule, "Back to States Rights." *Harper's Magazine*, 171:484, 490, September, 1935. See also "Some Legal and Practical Problems of the Interstate

Compact." *Yale Law Journal,* 45:326-27, footnote 15, December, 1935; E. S. Corwin, "Lessons of the Colorado River Compact." *National Municipal Review,* 16:459, July, 1927; and see Amry Vandenbosch, "Regions versus States." *Kentucky Law Journal,* 21:432, May, 1933.

[2] See "Some Legal and Practical Problems of the Interstate Compact." *Yale Law Journal,* 45:326-27, footnote 15, December, 1935; Lewis W. Douglas, *The Liberal Tradition; A Free People and a Free Economy* (New York: D. Van Nostrand, Inc., 1935), p. 124; William J. Donovan, "State Compacts As A Method of Settling Problems Common to Several States." *University of Pennsylvania Law Review,* 80: 5, November, 1931; William J. Donovan, "Regulation of Interstate Transmission of Gas and Electricity." *American Bar Association Reports,* 56:757-59, 1931; "Compacts Preferred." *State Government,* 7:140, July, 1934; *Congressional Record,* Vol. 78, pp. 12211, 12272.

[3] Dissenting in *New State Ice Co.* v. *Liebmann,* 285 U.S. 262, 311 (1932). See also Zechariah Chafee, Jr., "Interstate Interpleader." *Yale Law Journal,* 33: 685-727, May, 1924; Frankfurter and Landis, *op. cit.;* James M. Landis, "Report of Committee." *Handbook National Conference of Commissioners on Uniform State Laws,* 42:280, 281, 1932.

[4] Arthur W. Macmahon, "Compacts, Interstate." *Encyclopaedia of the Social Sciences,* IV, 111 (1931).

[5] "Interstate Co-operation," *Richmond Times-Dispatch,* June 14, 1949.

[6] See *supra,* Ch. II, Sections on jurisdiction and obligation of contracts.

[7] See *supra,* Ch. IV. [8] Dimock and Benson, *op. cit.,* p. 17. [9] *Ibid.,* p. 15.

[10] Macmahon, *op. cit.,* p. 111. "This will be true," he says, "even if interstate agreements go further than in the past in creating genuinely cohesive, autonomous agencies of regional jurisdiction. Pregnant possibilities of course exist."

[11] The first federal law on this subject was invalidated by the Supreme Court in *Panama Refining Co.* v. *Ryan,* 293 U.S. 388 (1935), on the ground that it delegated legislative power to the President without prescribing a standard to guide his exercise thereof. Congress subsequently enacted a law prohibiting interstate shipment of oil produced in excess of a state quota replacing the one invalidated by the Court. See 49 United States *Statutes at Large* 30, Ch. 18. Time limitations on the effectiveness of this act were removed and the act made "permanently effective" in 1942. 56 United States *Statutes at Large* 381, Ch. 436.

[12] Joseph J. Spengler, "The Economic Limitations to Certain Uses of Interstate Compacts." *American Political Science Review,* 31:51, February, 1937.

[13] *Ibid.*

[14] Dimock and Benson, *op. cit.,* p. 14. Dimock and Benson point out that "any problem that concerns political freedom, emotional and 'irrational' competition, rivalry, and even jealousy, will necessarily be difficult of solution. It will be difficult whether it is met by compact or by any other device for securing common action for a common end." *Ibid.,* p. 16.

[15] The idea that States are equal poses policy problems which must be resolved in consideration of whether to employ the compact method as a means to a given end. The National Resources Committee summarizes the antithesis between the assumptions of the regional "planner" and the "jurist" or "States' rights champion": "Briefly stated, the customary approach to prospective compacts is based upon the following assumptions: (1) Every State of the Union is sovereign, therefore (2) every State is equal, therefore (3) every State should get as much out of what is to be settled, or to be divided, as any other State entering into the

proposed compact. These assumptions may be good jurisprudence and the proper bases of comity, but considerable question arises concerning their realism and social desirability. The unequal distribution of natural resources, of climate, of economic advantage, or of transportation facilities, with their resulting effects upon population concentration, wealth, and cultural opportunity, challenges these juristic and artificial hypotheses. In short, the assumptions of planning, chief of which is that resources, physical and human, should be used to the best social advantage irrespective of artificially established interests or boundaries—these assumptions quite naturally come into conflict with certain governmental theories." National Resources Committee, *op. cit.*, pp. 50-51. The "regional" planner would develop the physical and human resources of the country at the points at which the maximum social advantage would be secured. The Committee points out that the State is the "dominant symbol" under the compact method, while perhaps it would be preferable to substitute for it the concept of regionalism.

[16] Soule, *op. cit.*, p. 490. Mr. Soule ignores the regional character of some problems and the necessary diversity of treatment to meet diverse needs.

[17] Harold J. Laski, *The American Democracy* (New York: The Viking Press, 1948), p. 156.

[18] See *supra,* Ch I. [19] See *supra,* Ch. I.

[20] Dimock and Benson, *op. cit.*, p. 16. The Committee on Interstate Compacts of the Conference of Commissioners on Uniform State Laws in their 1921 report stressed the need for uniformity in commercial law. They proposed the use of compacts in connection with the adoption of uniform state laws, moreover, to restrain the States from amending them except in unison.

[21] See *supra.*, Ch. II, pp. 64-66, for treatment of *Kentucky* v. *Indiana,* 281 U.S. 163 (1930), in which the Supreme Court decreed that Indiana must perform her contractural obligation incurred in the Indiana-Kentucky agreement to build a bridge across the Ohio River. Professor Macmahon cites an example to point the "important lesson of the utility of a carefully considered formal agreement instead of reliance merely on concert effected through concurrent legistlation. The Delaware River bridge at Philadelphia was built by a joint commission on the basis of laws passed by Pennsylvania and New Jersey in 1919. Congress sanctioned it as a bridge project (1921, 41 Stat. 1101); it was financed by the states separately. In 1925, shortly before its completion, Pennsylvania declared by law that it should be free. New Jersey, alleging that its bonds had assumed tolls, countered by attempting to stop construction. Pennsylvania began a suit but early in the following year paved the way for an agreement by repealing its declaration against tolls." Macmahon, *op. cit.*, p. 111.

[22] Dimock and Benson, *op. cit.*, p. 16. This view is corroborated by that of the Technical Committee on Regional Planning of the National Resources Committee: "When the problem is a continuing and complex one, the compact method is not only ill-adapted to the planning function but it leaves much to be desired from the standpoint of effective administration. It is a well-known fact, applicable to other forms of administration as well as business management, that successful administration requires adequate authority and opportunity for initiative, flexibility, and even experimentation. The more complex the economic or social problem, the more necessary are the last-mentioned administrative attributes. But autonomous administration is far from characteristic of the compact method; it is the principal difference between the compact and the regional development authority represented by the T. V. A." National Resources Committee, *op. cit.*, p. 41.

[23] *Ibid.*, p. 51. [24] Dimock and Benson, *op. cit.*, p. 10.

[25] National Resources Committee, *op. cit.*, p. 51.

[26] Dimock and Benson, *op. cit.*, p. 21.

[27] "Ancillary federal control can actively insure the effectiveness of compacts. A federal law might very well be enacted under which a state participating in a compact would be permitted to apply the standards set by the agreement to goods coming from without the state. Minimum-wage compacts, for example, might thus be made with less fear of unfair competition from sweatshop states." *Ibid.*, p. 18. See *supra*, Ch. VI, for another example.

[28] *The Book of the States, 1950-51,* 8:23-24.

[29] See W. Brooke Graves, *Uniform State Action* (Chapel Hill, N. C.: University of North Carolina Press, 1934), pt. IV, "Uniformity Through Judicial Cooperation."

[30] The Uniform Negotiable Instruments Act, for example, has been adopted in all the States. See Graves, *Uniform State Action,* pp. 43-45, for classification of uniform acts by sections showing number of adoptions.

[31] See *supra,* Ch. II, p. 36, for treatment of reciprocal legislation and the Compact Clause in *Virginia* v. *Tennessee.* For treatments of these methods of interstate cooperation and of means whereby the Federal Government copes with regional problems, see Graves, *Uniform State Action*; Dimock and Benson, *op. cit.*; National Resources Committee, *op. cit.*; and "The Laws of the States and the Various Means for Bringing Them Into Harmony." *State Government.*

[32] See *supra,* Chs. II and III.

[33] Macmahon, *op. cit.*, p. 111.

Chapter VII

CONCLUSIONS

From the foregoing study of the Compact Clause there emerges a picture of the compact device showing it to possess certain basic attributes. These attributes are significant for the determination of the possible role of the compact device in the federal system.

The compact is contractual in character. The treatment of a compact as a contract within the meaning of the contract impairment clause of the Constitution has its advantages and disadvantages, the former as to enforcement, and the latter as to inflexibility, rendering the compact device desirable for some applications and undesirable for others. Hence the device must be confined to appropriate subject matter. It is admirably suited for use in those fields of interstate cooperative action in which rigidity is desirable if not indispensable. Conversely, it is ill-suited for fields in which its use can mean strait-jacketed administration, prescription of standards on the level of the "lowest common denominator," and, in time, "ossified" arrangements. From this it follows that it is well-adapted for the solution of problems which can be settled "once and for all" but must be considered carefully and compared with alternative methods for use in connection with continuing functions.

Whether a compact can or cannot be enforced has real significance for the utility of the device. The obligation of the compact, which the Court once said "is 'the law which binds the parties to perform their agreement,'" is enforceable. Failure on the part of one State to fulfill the terms of a compact with another could be expected to lead to a suit within the original jurisdiction of the Supreme Court to secure the performance of the compact. The question of enforcement of an interstate compact is equivalent in the final analysis to the question of the power of the Supreme Court to enforce a judgment rendered by it against a State of the Union. Certain elements relative to the general question of enforcement of a judgment against a State are disposed of by the Court's holding ending the *Virginia* v. *West Virginia* series. The Court concluded that the right to enforce its judgment is inherent in the judicial power and is operative against a State which has consented in adoption of the Constitution to suit by another State. That judgment may be enforced against the State, *qua* State, and is operative upon its governmental agencies and its property, whether used for governmental purposes or held in a proprietary capacity. Congress possesses the two-fold power (1) to force the State's compliance with the judgment of the Court rendered in the constitutional exercise of the judicial power and (2) to add to existing judicial remedies to enable the Court to meet the problem precipitated by the judicial duty of enforcing its judgment against a State in such circumstances. And with respect to interstate compacts for the validity of which the consent of Congress is necessary, the power to see to the compact's enforcement, once it has become operative by the will of Congress, is implicit in the congressional power to assent.

The Court certainly asserted there its power to enforce its decree against a "sovereign" State, and its failure to indicate the specific means by which enforcement would be achieved is of little import. Indeed, no State has ever persisted in its refusal to obey a Supreme Court decision in an interstate suit. In the light of experience, the argument as to the "unenforceability of compacts" has been overemphasized.

This, of course, is not to say that effectiveness of the method can always be insured by a judicial decree to enforce compliance; for often effectiveness depends upon other factors, such as the spirit of compliance, the character of administration, and the participation of all the States necessary to the success of the compact.

A primary consideration in connection with enforcement is whether questions arising under interstate compacts can be brought before the federal judiciary and hence removed from state courts which as state instrumentalities might conceivably be interested in the outcome of the case. As a result of the chain of cases dealing with jurisdictional questions in respect to compacts, it would seem that almost any case involving a compact could be removed from a state court to the federal judiciary. The Court has held that construction of an interstate compact sanctioned by Congress in conformity with the constitutional requirement involves a federal "title, right, privilege or immunity" which, when "specially set up and claimed" under the United States Constitution in a state court, may be reviewed by the Supreme Court.

The compact device is the one method of interstate cooperative action which comes before a representative body of the nation for consideration in the light of broad public policy. The requirement of congressional consent affords Congress an opportunity to view the compact's projected treatment of regional problems with respect to its bearing on the welfare of the nation as a whole. Congress is the proper judge as to when and how its consent should be given. Moreover, the congressional power to consent includes the power to stipulate conditions upon which consent will be granted.

To be sure, the cases indicate a relaxation in the application of the requirement of congressional consent. Supreme Court dicta and state court decisions indicate that consent need not be given at all to agreements that can in no respect concern the United States. The Supreme Court, however, has been careful to cover under the consent requirement any combination tending to the increase of political power in the States which might encroach upon or interfere with the just supremacy of the United States.

Relaxation of the consent requirement would seem desirable from the viewpoint of rendering the compact somewhat less formal and reducing the inordinate length of time required for a compact's consummation. On the other hand, the dangerous potentialities of an apparently innocuous interstate arrangement might escape the attention of Congress. Moreover, if the resultant pact were rendered less enforceable, which, however, is doubtful in that it would retain its contractual character, the device might have lost its most valuable element for some uses. The courts might hold consent implicit in silence, using an argument somewhat analogous to the maxim that what the sovereign permits it commands. At least the Supreme Court has held that consent need not be express but may reasonably be implied.

The compact device is one of the elements in the "process which is crisscrossing all political boundaries with the lines of functional union." Aside from action by the Federal Government or by the States in conjunction with the Federal Government, it is, as indicated, the only element which is subjected to scrutiny in the light of broad public policy by a representative body of the whole nation. At the same time it is one method of tackling supra-state, sub-national problems which is compatible with the "principles of States' rights." In view of these considerations, its use would seem desirable wherever it appears applicable. That use may, indeed, be essential to preservation of the vitality and potency of the States and to avoidance of an overladen general government. And both of these may be essential to efficiency and to freedom. Certainly they are essential to federalism of the United States pattern.

INDEX

DATE DUE